Superstar Sales
Manager's Secrets

Revised Edition

Superstar Sales Manager's Secrets

Revised Edition

By

Barry Farber

CAREER PRESS

THE CAREER PRESS, INC.
Franklin Lakes, NJ

SUPERSTAR SALES MANAGER'S SECRETS, REVISED EDITION
EDITED AND TYPESET BY NICOLE DEFELICE
Cover design by Johnson Design
Printed in the U.S.A. by Book-mart Press

To order this title, please call toll-free 1-800-CAREER-1 (NJ and
Canada: 201-848-0310) to order using VISA or MasterCard, or for
further information on books from Career Press.

The Career Press, Inc., 3 Tice Road, PO Box 687,
Franklin Lakes, NJ 07417
www.careerpress.com

Library of Congress Cataloging-in-Publication Data

Farber, Barry J.
    Superstar sales manager's secrets / by Barry Farber.— Rev. ed.
        p. cm.
    Includes index.
    ISBN 1-56414-659-6 (pbk.)
        1. Sales management. I. Title.

HF5438.4 .F37 2003
658.8—dc21   2002041249

DEDICATION

To Sensei Mark Walker—a great leader who lives what he teaches, trains in the trenches, and drives home the fundamentals every day.

ACKNOWLEDGMENTS

Special thanks to all the superstars who gave their time and shared their insight.

I'd especially like to thank: Marylou Armendinger, Jorja Coulter, Don Duncan, Michael Liess, Rich Luisi, Charles McLane, Robert Means, Jim Miller, Todd Rose, Debbie Qaqish, Jim Smith, and Larry Stein.

And to Sharyn Kolberg with great appreciation for her patient listening and her excellent editorial skills.

Special thanks to the Career Press staff: to Ron Fry, Michael Lewis, Nicole DeFelice, and Stacey A. Farkas for their support, enthusiasm, publishing excellence, and outstanding work and quality in production.

CONTENTS

INTRODUCTION

When I was a sales manager, the best rep I had on my team was not the most experienced, the most knowledge-able, or the most skilled. In fact, he was kind of rough around the edges. I wasn't concerned about that; I knew he could be fine-tuned in areas that needed improvement. So why was he my best rep? He wasn't afraid to go out there, make the cold calls, seek out new accounts, and sell them. I wished I had 1,000 reps like him.

The information in this book has been culled from my own experience in the field and feedback from more than 10,000 sales managers. Whenever I ask a manager why a sales rep fails to succeed, I get the same answer: *lack of activity.* This is usually a result of a lack of confidence in their skills and product knowledge, which causes them to be uncomfortable prospecting and making cold calls.

That's where *Superstar Sales Manager's Secrets* comes in. This is not only a guide to coaching and training your reps in the skills they need, it's a handbook full of practical tools and motivational strategies to help your reps generate activity and get the business.

As managers, most of us have come into that position from a sales background, where closing a sale provided one of life's greatest highs. Now we have to get that high vicariously through our reps, watching them become successful on their own. However, that can be a great reward. If you can look down the road and realize that you're changing the lives of the people on your team, that should be the major reason why you became a manager. The thrill is no longer in the individual sale; it's in the team's success. The times when you have to sit back and watch your reps fail are frustrating. But it's part of the job—to let go of the leadership position, where you show them how to do it—to letting them show you how they do it.

The information in this book is real-world and result-oriented. It's perfect as a guidebook for the new manager, or as a source of new ideas for the more experienced. This book is meant to be referred to often. Adapt its ideas to your particular business and personal style. Copy the forms and checklists for your own use.

Be passionate about your work, and remember that enthusiasm is catching. Be proud of what you do, and be proud of what you have to share with your team. Let your effort and activity levels be a model for your reps to follow. And remember these words from philosopher Orison Swett Marden:

"People who have accomplished work worthwhile have had a very high sense of the way to do things. They have not been content with mediocrity... They always pushed things that came to their hands a little higher up, this little farther on, that counts in the quality of life's work."

CHAPTER 1

WHAT SALES MANAGERS ARE MADE OF

The Sales Manager Everyone Hates to Work For

One of the first things you become aware of when you become a sales manager is that you have many roles to play. At various times (and often all at the same time), you are a time management supervisor, a meeting planner, a contest creator, a report generator, a talent scout, a disciplinarian, a coach, a salesperson, a customer service specialist, a trainer, and a psychiatrist. All these roles together, well-executed, make for a great manager—one whose main purpose is to get the best out of his or her people.

That is the bottom-line goal of every manager—to build a strong, confident, productive team. It's not always an easy job, and there are many factors that block our success in that effort. Based on interviews with top salespeople around the country, the following portrait of the sales manager everyone hates to work for was created.

Ever hear this horror story? A sales rep, feeling a little shaky about closing a deal, asks his manager to come along and give him a hand. The manager, basically a paper-pushing desk-sitter, agrees to go. On the way to the call, he asks a few questions, then gets distracted talking about big accounts he landed in the past. When they get to the call, it's obvious to the customer that the manager knows nothing about his business, and the rep and manager leave without getting the business.

"Boy," the manager says to the rep as they walk out the door, "you sure blew that one!"

Not only did this manager lose a sale, he lost all credibility with his sales force. (Have no doubt, this sales rep will tell everyone on the team.) A good manager, one who's out in the field all the time, wouldn't make this kind of mistake. Which is not to say that great managers are infallible. It's just that if they do make a mistake, they're the first to admit it. Every sales rep, when asked what kind of a manager he or she would most like to work for, has the same thought: someone who's honest and up-front, who gives his all to the job and to his people, and who doesn't have time for games and blame.

Unfortunately, horror-story managers do exist. Just so you'll recognize one should you ever run into a bad sales manager, here are the 10 most common characteristics of the manager everyone hates to work for:

1. **Low energy, low enthusiasm.** Mr. Negative never gets excited about anything. He's unhappy in his job, and shares that information freely. He's constantly depressed—and so is his team.

2. **No vision.** He sets no goals for himself or his team. He gives the reps one direction on Monday morning, and by Tuesday afternoon he's saying something completely different.

3. **Willing to settle for average performance.** He "hasn't got time" to work with reps or develop their potential. He doesn't expect much from his team, and he doesn't get much.

4. **Takes credit for everything.** This manager's ego needs constant stroking. So every sale becomes his own, no matter how much or how little he had to do with it. He takes full credit for his reps' successes.

5. **A finger-pointer.** When something goes wrong, he's the first one to point out who did it and exactly what went wrong (unless the mistake was his). He is quick to point out a rep's shortcomings, and slow to offer any suggestions or solutions.

6. Glued to his desk. He's a real nine-to-fiver who is steeped in paperwork and seldom gets out in the field. He's always exhorting his reps to start out early and stay late—but is not willing to do the same.

7. **Cares more about getting his commission than about his people.** He's more interested in the short-term results than in the long-term growth of his people.

8. **Lack of communication skills.** He knows how to tell his reps what's wrong, but doesn't know how to teach new skills. His listening skills

leave a lot to be desired, and his reps don't feel comfortable asking him for advice.

9. **Lets his "friends" stop pulling their weight.** He has favorites on the team, who take advantage of their friendship and get away with low activity and poor results, causing resentment and discontent among the other reps.

10. **Doesn't stand behind his team.** He's only interested in impressing the corporate bigwigs. He doesn't realize that the success of a sales manager is in direct proportion to his team's results.

Jim Smith has been a top field sales manager at Mid American Waste Systems for over 20 years. Before he came there, however, he worked for one of those horror-story managers described. "The thing I hated most," says Jim, "was that I had to adapt to a style that I wasn't comfortable with. The manager's style was very technical and manipulative. You had to follow an exact questioning process, trying to force the prospect to answer the way you wanted."

The other frustrating aspect of this misguided manager was that he was quick to criticize. "There was no system for measuring what you were doing well," says Jim. "He never complimented anyone; he always looked for what we were doing wrong." Now that Smith is a manager himself, he's especially sensitive to his reps' various selling styles. "If a sales rep has to adapt to someone else's style," he says, "you can read it in his face and hear it in the way he stutters over his words. When he's got his own style, he's confident and can come across clearly and succinctly."

Fortunately, most managers *don't* fit this profile. There are a lot of enthusiastic, caring, and supportive team leaders. One such manager was described to me by Todd Rose of Gestetner Office Products. Rose, who started at the company with no sales experience and ascended to the number two Gestetner sales rep in the country, attributes most of his success to his manager, Greg Gondek.

"Greg is always there when you need him," says Rose. "He makes you work your butt off, but he's not constantly looking over your shoulder. He lets you go out and prove that you can do it yourself. But if you have a problem, you know you always have somebody in your corner you can rely on, and you know he's going to help you out."

Rose also notes that what makes Gondek a good manager is that he practices what he preaches. "If you go into an account with Greg by your side, there's a 99 percent chance you're going to walk out with an order," he says. Gondek shares his knowledge, experience, and new ideas with his team every Monday morning, and gets his reps fired up for the week ahead.

He is, in fact, the opposite of the horror-story manager.

- ✬ He respects his reps as individuals, and allows them to use their personal selling styles.
- ✬ He lets his reps know what's expected of them, expects them to do their best, and is willing to lend a hand if there's a problem that needs solving.
- ✬ Most of all, he's interested in the long-term growth of his team—he makes an investment in his people, knowing it's going to be paid back tenfold.

The manager everyone hates to work for is the one whose personal interests come before his interest in the team. The *great* manager, the one every rep loves to work for, puts his team first and lives by this principle:

You elevate your own success when you elevate the success of others.

Traits of a Successful Manager

Where do successful managers come from? Most come from the ranks of successful salespeople. But that doesn't necessarily make them great managers. The best take the skills they've learned out in the field, and add the traits of effective leadership. The following are eight traits that distinguish the best from the rest:

1. **They develop a genuinely positive attitude.** A positive attitude is more than just thinking good thoughts. Successful managers believe that a person's attitude can make all the difference. They believe in possibilities; that most problems can be solved. They are enthusiastic about their jobs and about their lives. They know that how they act and react to various situations is a model for the team's actions and reactions. Because enthusiasm is contagious, a manager with a positive attitude usually leads a team with a positive attitude.

2. **They display a willingness to work toward what they want to achieve.** Successful managers know that nothing worthwhile is ever achieved without effort. They're willing to do whatever it takes to make their team successful. They spend time in the field with reps,

and do not expect their people to do anything they wouldn't do themselves.

3. **They understand that everyone makes mistakes—and they know how to help reps learn from mistakes and failures.** They have been out in the field themselves, and know what it's like to face rejection. But they are not defeated by it. They expect it as a part of life, know there is a lesson to be learned in every setback, and pass this philosophy on to their reps.

4. **They surround themselves with positive ideas and role models.** Successful managers believe in the saying "You become what you think about." They know the importance of a positive environment, and keep reminders of their success and their teams' success visible. They seek out mentors whose wisdom and experience can help them achieve their goals, and they encourage their reps to do the same.

5. **They never stop learning.** They are constantly looking to improve. They do not assume that because they've reached a certain level of success they can stop learning. They study their skills and their industry. They keep their minds open to new techniques and share their knowledge with their team. If managers aren't learning and growing, they're not just standing still, they're going backwards.

6. **They are passionate about what they do.** If you love your work, it's not hard labor. If the sales manager loves her job, there's a much better chance her reps will love theirs.

Passion fires you up. It produces energy and gives you a sense of unlimited potential and possibility. Passion and enthusiasm are transferred to the entire sales team. If a manager is negative, everyone else will be pulled down. How do successful managers maintain a realistically positive attitude? Great leaders are great readers: They read everything they can find about their crafts and industries. They seek out mentors whose wisdom and experience can help them achieve their goals, and they encourage their reps to do the same. They surround themselves with high-quality people.

7. **They set goals.** They focus on what they want to achieve, establish priorities, and know what they have to do in order to keep moving forward. They spend time with their reps, developing goals that are in the best interest of the individual reps, the team, and the company. They are able to set realistic, achievable goals for themselves and their team, and they keep those goals visible so everyone knows the targets they are expected to reach.

8. **They enjoy giving back to others.** The main reason for becoming a manager is so you can use your skills, knowledge, and experience to help others achieve. Successful managers are grateful for what they have been able to achieve, and are happy to help others do the same. They agree with William H. Danforth, who more than 70 years ago wrote in his inspirational book, *I Dare You!*:

"Catch a passion for helping others and a richer life will come back to you."

Your role as a leader is to encourage your people to succeed. There may be substantial monetary rewards in being a great sales leader, but the greatest reward is having helped others reach their goals. Our material possessions won't really matter once we're gone. Our greatest legacy is the people we've helped build, who are left to build others in the same way.

CHAPTER 2

HOW TO HIRE EFFECTIVELY

The Role of Talent Scout

Of all the roles a manager plays, one of the most crucial is one that gets pushed to the side until an emergency arises—the role of talent scout. Big-league teams don't stop looking for new players just because they have a star pitcher on the team. They always have someone out there watching the minor leagues, traveling to small towns across the country searching for undiscovered talent.

With all the roles you have to play, and all the tasks that go into each of those roles, you might not feel you have the time to be a full-time talent scout as well. However, there is one important factor that can make each and every one of those tasks a hundred times easier: hiring quality people in the first place.

That's the reason why hiring is one of the first subjects covered in this book. If you hire the wrong person, it doesn't matter how much training, coaching, or counseling you try. It doesn't matter how much of a motivating environment you create. It doesn't matter how many probationary periods you allow. You're going against the grain, and it will be an uphill struggle all the way, until eventually the wrong hire leaves, either by your choice or his.

That situation always takes an emotional toll on a manager, and on a team. But it takes an even larger financial toll. It can cost anywhere from $10,000 to $100,000 a year when we hire the wrong person. And that's not only measured in salary, commission, and draw. It includes intangibles as well: the time you spend trying to train and coach, the time taken away from helping other reps, and the damage to the wrong hire's territory. Once you realize the expense of hiring the wrong person, you realize why it's so critical to make good hiring choices.

The success of a sales manager is in direct proportion to the success of the team. Here are some effective techniques for recruiting the type of people you need to make a dynamic sales team.

Always be recruiting

Unfortunately, most managers start recruiting when someone is leaving. That often means they settle for second best, or end up with someone just to fill a gap. This can be a costly error. Think about the impact an incompetent rep can have on a territory. Customers will find it hard to trust your company name and the next rep who comes to call. If you're always recruiting, you have a file full of prequalified candidates you can call upon when necessary.

Reject hiring myths and stereotypes

The best salesperson you can hire is an aggressive extrovert with 10 years of sales experience, right? Although many managers think so, it isn't always true. In a study of more than 100,000 sales professionals, there was no difference in the success rate between introverts and extroverts.

26

In fact, many customers felt more comfortable with introverts, and said they were more trustworthy and consultative. A sales rep's years of experience is not an effective indicator of success, either. Some inexperienced reps with a great desire to learn do better on the job than reps who've "been around" and "know all there is to know" about sales.

Carry the recruiting message with you

One easy way to sustain ongoing recruiting is to carry a set of business cards with the following message on the back: "I was very impressed with your service. Please call me if you're ever looking for a job." Whenever you're in a restaurant or store, and you come in contact with anyone doing his or her job exceptionally well, pass out a card. Look for vendors who come to you. Day to day, as a manager, you probably deal with vendors all the time. If someone impresses you, ask her if she likes her job, and if she'd ever consider working for someone else. By handing out this card to someone who exhibits a positive attitude, energy, and enthusiasm—when she doesn't know she's being observed—you not only decrease your recruiting costs, you increase your opportunity for getting qualified people.

Set up a computer bulletin board

At Val-Pak, franchise owners are constantly encouraged to establish ongoing recruiting programs. "We stress to the owners they need to let everyone know they're always interested in talking to a potential sales representative," says Marylou Armendinger, vice president of Network Development. "If you're constantly recruiting, you always have a backlog of prescreened candidates to pull from." To help franchisees in this effort, Val-Pak set up its own computer bulletin board so that managers from across the country can swap ideas and techniques for successful recruiting.

Encourage current employees to recommend new hires

No one knows your company and your team as well as the people who are presently employed by your firm. They may have friends or acquaintances they feel would be a perfect fit for your organization. Any employee (not just the sales reps) should get monetary compensation if the person they recommend stays more than 90 days. This is incentive for the employees to recommend qualified people they feel can do the job.

Enlist college interns

In addition to any regular recruiting you might do on a college campus, check with the placement office about intern programs. Interns are usually college juniors or seniors who work for you for free or for a nominal amount (enough to pay for transportation expenses, for instance). In exchange, they get work experience, and often college credits. And, if the intern works out well, you may be able to offer a job (after graduation, of course) to someone who's already been trained for it!

Advertise

Advertising can be an effective medium for generating candidates. But when you're running a general ad (for example: "Marketing rep wanted. Potential for making lots of money. Great opportunity for career advancement."), you run the risk of getting a high number of unqualified responses. Your ad should be customized to your industry and your company so that it attracts the right candidates. Advertising is especially effective if you advertise in trade publications for reps with specific industry or product knowledge.

Measure motivation before you hire

If you ask managers about the most important attributes they look for in a job candidate, *motivation* and *desire* would probably be high on their list, along with *energetic, highly competitive,* and *hardworking.* The common denominator in all these attributes is effort. Most sales managers will hire a rep without experience or industry knowledge if they're willing to put in 110 percent. Of course, sales managers aren't the only people concerned with finding motivated people. As a squadron commander and flight instructor, Lt. Col. Dennis Krembel of the United States Air Force must seek out the "best of the best" for the defense of our country. When I asked Lt. Col. Krembel what he looks for in a "top gun," he replied, "...one thing I always look for is desire. In many cases, I'll even take desire over talent. If I look at one person who's got the talent, and at another person who's got the desire... I'll take the person who's willing to go that extra measure... I'll probably invest more time with that person because I know he's going to go farther in all the things that he needs to be successful."

There's nothing worse than hiring someone and investing energy, time, and money, only to see it go to waste several months later for lack of internal motivation and a strong work ethic. If there was some way to measure a sales rep's effort before he or she was hired, we'd all have winning teams. Unfortunately, we can't predict the future 100 percent. But actions speak louder than words. Here are several practical ideas that will dramatically increase your hiring success by measuring effort, creativity, and desire before you hire:

⭐ **Telephone prescreen.** Start evaluating a candidate during your first telephone conversation, even before you've met them in person.

What is your impression? Does the candidate seem enthusiastic? Does she listen? Is she pushy or overly aggressive? Is the conversation pleasant, yet professional? Write down your impressions of the conversation, and see if you still feel the same way after you meet face to face.

★ **30-day action plan.** Ask candidates to come back after the first interview with a detailed outline of what they would do to be successful the first month on the job. This will not only evaluate the effort they spend thinking about their activities and goals, but it will also give you an idea of what they think it takes to get the job done. If you decide to hire, not only do you already have goals set for the first 30 days, but these are goals that have come from the reps themselves—and when they say it, they own it.

★ **Why them? Why us?** Have candidates list 10 reasons why they feel qualified for the job and what they can offer your company. Then have them list several reasons why they want to work within your industry, for your specific company, and why in sales. These questions will not only tell you how much time and effort they put into this assignment, but also why they think they're qualified, and what attracted them to this position in the first place.

★ **The presentation.** Suppose you've interviewed a candidate you like very much. How can you measure both his skill level and his motivation before you hire? After the interview, hand him one of your product brochures. Don't give him any more information, but ask him to come back in a day or so to sell you the product. You want to see how much effort he puts into finding out about your company, product, needs, etc. Then, when he comes back, you can measure the following:

☆ Amount of research, time, and effort put into the presentation.

☆ Creativity. Is there anything unique and potentially effective about his approach?

☆ Selling skills. This is the perfect time to measure sales skills, from start to finish.

If you're interviewing an experienced sales rep, you might ask him to sell you the product he's currently handling, you can still use your product as part of this exercise to measure preparation and effort. Of course, if the candidate doesn't come back to sell you the product, you've saved yourself a lot of unnecessary time and effort.

★ **In-house observation.** After the first or second interview, have the candidate travel in the field for half a day with an experienced sales rep. Make sure you select one of your better reps and have him or her make a typical day of calls—canvassing, customer visits, appointments, and cold calls. Allow the candidate to observe what it's really like to work for your company. The candidate may open up to the sales rep (a peer) about questions and concerns that might never come up during the office interview. You might also have your rep ask the candidate to take a cold call himself. This can be an excellent measure of the candidate's composure under pressure, as well as basic selling skills.

Bob Means, president of Oxicon Corp., supports the use of this technique. "Having the candidate travel with a rep is a great chance to expose the candidate to a realistic view of the job," he says, "and at the same time it gives your current employee some recognition as a role model." It's also an opportunity for you to get another person's input. Ask your rep if he or she thinks the candidate would be good for the job, and why.

Resume Dos and Don'ts

The resume is usually what gives you the first impression of a candidate. Although sometimes we put too much stock in what's on the paper and not enough on the candidate's true potential, a resume can give you hints and red flag warnings. Here are some key elements to look for when reviewing resumes:

✯ **Does the resume include accomplishments?** You're not just looking for a chronological list of jobs. The candidate should include what she accomplished at each of her jobs, including her rankings. If they're not on the resume, ask the candidate what they were and why they were not included.

✯ **Does the resume show a pattern of success?** Did each successive job mean a higher level of income and responsibility? Was the candidate simply jumping from one job to the next? During the interview, you'll want to ask the candidate why she left her most recent position.

✯ **Are there any unexplained gaps between jobs?** If there is a fairly long gap between the end of one job and the beginning of the next, you want to know what the candidate was doing during that time. If it took that long to get a new job, why? And if the candidate was engaged in some other occupation or activity during the gap, you want to know what that activity was.

✰ **Is the resume neat and free of typos?** If the resume is extremely messy and difficult to read, it can be an indication that the candidate doesn't really care how she represents herself. This is not a good sign, as she will be representing your company if she is hired, and you want your company to be represented well.

Resume Cover Sheet

Because you are always recruiting, even when you don't have an immediate opening, you need some way of keeping track of your impressions of people you've interviewed. Use the form on the next page to record your impressions from every aspect of the interviewing process. Make notes to yourself of questions you may want to ask in a future interview, and rank the candidate. Write the number (between 1 and 10) on the upper right-hand corner of the page so that it's easily visible. File the sheets in rank order, with the 10s on top, then the 9s, and so on, and call on the top-ranked candidates when you have an opening on your team.

Resume Cover Sheet

Candidate:_____ Overall Rank: ____

Date of Interview: _____	Time: _____

Comment and questions from:

Resume:

Telephone call:

Application:

Interviews by others in the company:

Observation ratings (1 = poor / 10 = excellent):

1. Appearance   1 2 3 4 5 6 7 8 9 10
2. Ability to establish
   and build rapport   1 2 3 4 5 6 7 8 9 10
3. Communication skills   1 2 3 4 5 6 7 8 9 10
4. Asked relevant questions   1 2 3 4 5 6 7 8 9 10
5. Assertiveness   1 2 3 4 5 6 7 8 9 10
6. Overall rating   1 2 3 4 5 6 7 8 9 10

Interviewing Your Way to Hiring Success

The interviewing process can pose particular problems for the sales manager. A potentially exciting candidate may know how to sell himself really well at an interview—but may never live up to his promise when it comes to day-to-day field work. That means you've got to dig beneath the surface—probe and clarify until you're convinced this candidate would be a valuable asset to your team. Here are some techniques you can use to improve the quality of the interviewing process:

Explain the interview procedure before you begin

Tell candidates that this is an informal interview, and that you are going to ask a few questions. Let them know they'll have an opportunity a little later to ask questions about the job and the company. Never explain to the candidate what you're looking for in a rep before you ask them questions. If you say up front, for instance, that you're looking for someone who is a really good closer, you can bet that before the interview is over, the candidate will describe himself as "a really good closer." Have candidates describe themselves before you reveal your ideal hire.

Ask open-ended questions

Naturally, you want to find out as much as you can in the brief amount of time you have for each interview. You want to hear what the candidates have to say, but you also want to hear how they say it. They're going to be talking to customers all the time, so you want to make sure they have excellent communication skills. Ask questions that get the candidates talking. Create open-ended questions that start with the following:

Tell me about...
Explain...
Expand on...
Share with me...
Can you give me more detail...
Can you describe...

Ask probing questions

Conducting an interview is very much like selling to a customer. You want to find out as much about the customer (in this case, the job candidate) as possible. The most important thing you can do in an interview is to ask one open-ended question, followed by two or three related probing questions. Dig into the information you get so that you can make a realistic evaluation of the candidate. Too often, managers make a list of questions and simply go from one to the next without getting complete answers to any of them.

Key qualifying questions

Here are some of the most important questions you can ask during an interview:

Why do you want to work in this industry? For this company? In sales? You want to find out the candidates' motivation and interest in your type of product or service, what research, if any, they've done about your company prior to the interview, and what attracted them to the field of sales.

If I were to talk to your previous manager and ask what your strong points are, what would she tell me? There are two reasons for phrasing the question this way: 1. Most candidates have already prepared a list of their strong points to tell you. Asking in this manner gets them thinking more objectively, giving you feedback from their manager's point of view, not theirs; 2. It makes candidates wonder if you might be planning to call their previous managers and ask this question—which means they'd better be honest in how they describe themselves.

If I were to talk to your previous manager and ask what your weak points are, what would she tell me? If you simply ask for the candidates' weak points, they'll likely give you a positive negative such as "People say I'm too neat and organized." Once again, asking what their managers would say usually produces a more objective response.

Take me through your typical day of selling. Ask for an hour by hour overview, including what time they arrive, what they do during each part of the day, what time they leave work, etc. You want to find out how they set their schedules, how much preparation they put in, how much field work they perform, when they do paperwork—and get an overall feel for their work ethic.

Tell me about a recent account you lost and why you lost it. If the rep says, "I can't even think of one I've recently lost," you should be suspicious. A rep who generates a lot of activity also generates a lot of rejection, and should be able to give you examples of lost accounts. Follow up this question by asking, "What could you have done differently?" and, "What did you learn from that experience?"

Tell me about a recent success you had. You want to find out what type of approach usually works for this candidate. Here is another instance where you can follow up with, "What did you learn from that experience?"

Why are you leaving your present job? The reasons candidates offer will give you an idea of what they're looking for in a new job. For instance, if a candidate says, "My manager never spent any time with me," this could be a clue that this candidate prefers to work with hands-on support.

What are the attributes of a successful salesperson? You don't want to hear generalities such as professionalism or a neat appearance. You're looking for specifics, such as a positive attitude, generating activity, the ability to cold call, and persistence, etc.

Here are additional questions you might want to ask. Choose those that work best for you and your industry:

- ✯ *What motivates you about selling?*
- ✯ *What do you like least about selling?*
- ✯ *Do you win or lose most accounts you go after, and why?*
- ✯ *As your sales manager, what three things could I do to help you improve your sales?*
- ✯ *Who has been your best sales manager, and why?*
- ✯ *Who has been your worst sales manager, and why?*
- ✯ *How do you feel about paperwork? When do you do it?*
- ✯ *Where would you like to be in two years, five years, 10 years?*
- ✯ *What are some of your outside interests?*
- ✯ *Who are your role models, professionally and personally?*
- ✯ *Have you ever felt like giving up on an account? Did you? Why or why not?*
- ✯ *In what type of work environment do you feel most productive?*
- ✯ *What training or past experiences have contributed most to your professional or personal development?*

Give candidates a job description

Sometime during the interview (probably after candidates have answered questions about themselves and their work habits), give candidates a complete job description. You don't want to hire anybody under false pretenses. Tell them what your quotas are, how many cold calls they're expected to make, what kind of support they can expect, etc. Give candidates every opportunity to decide whether this is a job in which they would be happy and productive. The job description also sets up your expectations from the start, and these can be reviewed later on if the candidate is hired.

Try to sell candidates out of the job

Toward the end of the interview, say, "Based on what I've heard so far, I just don't feel you're qualified for this position." This is a test of candidates' skills. Are they willing to fight for the job? If they just take no for an answer, what will they do if a customer says, "I don't feel your product meets our needs"? Find out if they are willing to sell themselves.

Always interview candidates before or after working hours

You want to spend prime work time with your people. And if a candidate presently has a job, and is interviewing when he's supposed to be working, what does that say about his work ethic? Will he do the same when he's working for you?

Three to the fourth (3^4)

Here are four crucial steps to take while interviewing, each with three components to them:

1. *Always interview candidates three separate times.*
   The worst thing you can do is get excited about

a candidate and hire him on the spot. You might get carried away by a "hunch" that tells you this is the right person for the job, or simply because you like the candidate. But quick decisions can be costly, so be sure to ask key qualifying questions and take the steps mentioned earlier to measure motivation before you hire.

2. *Have three different people interview candidates.* The two other people could include your peer managers, your supervisor, the company owner or CEO, a service department manager—anyone whom you feel would be able to give you an objective opinion of the candidate and his or her sales potential. Don't tell them any of your feelings about this candidate because you don't want to influence their opinion in any way. Having other people interview the candidate serves two purposes: 1. You get other people's insight (they might pick up something you missed); and 2. It gives the job added value. If a candidate goes in for an interview and walks out with a job, what value will she place on it? The job will mean more if she feels she earned it.

Another way of doing this is to have two people (other than yourself) interviewing the candidate at the same time, asking questions from different categories. The first person might ask, "What are your goals?" The second person might follow that with, "What's the last sale you lost?" There are college courses and many books available on how to answer interview questions. The two-person technique is often a good way to find out how well candidates think on their feet, because that's what they're going to have to do on the job.

40

3. *Hold interviews in three different places.* People react differently in different environments. The first interview would naturally take place in your office. One could be conducted in the field when the candidate goes out with an experienced rep. The third could be in a restaurant, or in someone else's office. Never tell the candidate you want to meet with him to make him an offer. Say, "I need to see you one more time so I can make my decision." If things don't go well in the new environment, you won't be locked into a promise you made.

4. *Check at least three separate references.* The biggest mistake managers make is falling in love with a candidate who is just like them. You want to find out how the candidate functions in real-life selling situations. Call at least three people who can vouch for both the candidate's work ethic and personal integrity.

Telephone Reference Checks

Ask managers what they would change about their last hiring experience, and the most frequent answer you get is, "I would have checked the references." Managers tend to get excited about candidates who make a good impression. However, they may be leaving their old jobs because their production was not as good as the first impressions they are able to make. You may find that you can't call the candidate's present employer because he hasn't given notice yet. In that case, find out if you can call previous employers, and perhaps even a customer. Assure your candidate that all such calls will be kept confidential.

Here are three key questions you should be asking on a reference call:

1. *I'm interviewing Bill Smith for a position in our company as a sales representative selling computer systems. Do you feel Mr. Smith would be qualified for this job, and if so, why?* You want to let the reference know a little about the job so that he can make an evaluation based on what he knows about the candidate and his potential for success within your company.

2. *How long have you known this individual?* An opinion from someone who has known the candidate for six years would be weighted more heavily than an opinion from someone who has known the candidate for three months. You should get a red flag warning if a candidate gives you a number of references who have only known him for a short time. If possible, check with at least one person who has known the candidate for several years.

3. *"Knowing what you now know about this individual, would you rehire him?"* If the answer is no, there's probably a good reason why. Whichever answer you get, ask the reference to go into detail so that you can make an effective evaluation of the candidate.

Key Success Factors From Top Performers

The following is a list of key factors that sales reps need to exhibit in order to be successful. This list was gathered from top performers around the country in all areas of sales. Use this list as a guideline to see how your candidates measure up in each of these categories.

✯ Attitude.

✯ Enthusiasm.

★ Effort.

★ Availability.

★ Does the little things (goes beyond what's expected).

★ Professionalism (love and pride in profession).

★ Knows your customer's business.

★ Listens, listens, listens!

★ Sense of humor.

★ Goal-setting.

★ Follow-up.

★ Constant prospecting (referral selling).

★ Never stops learning.

★ Builds long-term relationships with customers.

★ Builds relationships with positive role models and mentors.

★ Earns the right to close.

★ Differentiates self through outrageous service.

When interviewing candidates, ask questions that will give you insight into each of these characteristics. For example:

How often do you keep in contact with your customers once the sale is made? (Follow-up.)

What would your customers say makes you stand out from other reps with whom they deal? (Differentiation through service.)

What was the last book you read on selling or customer service? (Never stops learning.)

Hiring Checklist

☑ **Always be recruiting.** Use these tips and techniques to keep your file full of potential candidates:

   ☆ Reject hiring myths and stereotypes.

   ☆ Print up and carry business cards with the message, "I was very impressed with your service. Please call me if you're ever looking for a job."

   ☆ Set up a computer bulletin board so that managers can share ideas and recruiting techniques.

   ☆ Reward current employees for recommending new hires who stay for at least 90 days.

   ☆ Utilize college interns whenever possible.

   ☆ Advertise in trade publications where you're more likely to attract qualified applications.

☑ **Measure motivation before you hire.** You can't predict the future, but you can hedge your bets by using these techniques to gauge effort, creativity, and desire:

   ☆ Keep notes of your impressions of candidates, beginning with your first phone conversation.

   ☆ Ask candidates to come back with a 30-day action plan describing the steps they would take to be successful on the job.

   ☆ Have candidates list 10 reasons why they are qualified for the job, and what they can offer your company.

☆ Measure motivation, creativity, and selling skills by having candidates return after the first interview to make a presentation and sell you your product or service.

☆ Send potential candidates out into the field with experienced reps to get a feel for the real-life aspects of the job.

☑ **Resume dos and don'ts.** Ask yourself four questions concerning a candidate's resume:

☆ Does the resume include accomplishments?

☆ Does the resume show a pattern of success?

☆ Are there any unexplained gaps between jobs?

☆ Is the resume neat and free of typos?

☑ **Resume cover sheet.** Use the resume cover sheet on page 34 to record your impressions of candidates, as well as any questions you may want to ask them in future interviews. Rank candidates from 1 to 10 (10 being the best), and file with the 10s on top so that you can pick from the best when you're in need of a new team member.

☑ **Interview your way to hiring success.** Here are some techniques you can use to improve the quality of your interviewing process:

☆ Explain the interviewing procedures before you begin.

☆ Ask open-ended questions that begin with:
Tell me about...
Explain....
Expand on...
Share with me...
Can you give me more details about...
Can you describe...

45

☆ Ask probing questions.

☆ Ask key qualifying questions.

☆ Be sure candidates have a complete job description.

☆ Tell candidates they're not qualified for the job, and see how they react.

☆ Schedule interviews before and after working hours.

☆ Use the three to the fourth principle:

1. Always interview candidates three separate times.

2. Have three different people interview candidates.

3. Hold interviews in three different places.

4. Check at least three separate references.

☑ **Telephone reference checks**. Here are three key questions you should be asking on a reference call:

1. I'm interviewing Bill Smith for a position in our company as a sales representative selling computer systems. Do you feel Mr. Smith would be qualified for this job, and if so, why?

2. How long have you known this individual?

3. Knowing what you now know about this individual, would you rehire him?

☑ **Key success factors from top performers.** Use this list of success factors gathered from top performers around the nation to create questions that elicit information and insight into the candidate's own potential for success:

☆ Attitude.

☆ Enthusiasm.

☆ Effort.

☆ Availability.

☆ Goes beyond what's expected.

☆ Professionalism.

☆ Knows customers' business.

☆ Listens.

☆ A sense of humor.

☆ Goal-setting.

☆ Follow-up.

☆ Constant prospecting.

☆ Never stops learning.

☆ Builds long-term relationships with customers.

☆ Builds relationships with positive role models and mentors.

☆ Earns the right to close.

☆ Differentiates self through outrageous service.

CHAPTER 3

THE SALES MANAGER'S ROLE

The managerial life is the broadest, the most demanding, by all odds the most comprehensive and the most subtle of all human activities. And the most crucial. A manager's function is to lead and move and bring out the latent capabilities—and dreams—of other human beings.

—David E. Lilienthal
Former chair, Tennessee Valley Authority

Being a sales manager is truly a difficult task. If you're like most managers, you came to this position because you had great success as a salesperson. But managing your accounts is not the same as managing your team. As a salesperson, you could easily measure your success through numbers of calls made and products sold. As a manager, your success is measured by the success of others. That's not always an easy transition to make. However, it is ultimately a rewarding one. Being a sales manager provides you with the opportunity to share your knowledge and expertise, and to help others grow professionally and personally. As the saying goes, when you elevate the success of others, you elevate your own as well.

Today, salespeople respect those managers who are tuned into their key needs, and who are willing to go out into the field with them and give them the training they want. The best managers are available whenever needed, but know when to let go and let a rep experience success (and perhaps failure) on his or her own. The way to accomplish this is to:

- ✯ **Spend time with your people.** Get to know their strengths and weaknesses, as well as their selling environment.

- ✯ **Lead by example.** Show your team that you don't expect them to do anything you're not willing to do yourself.

- ✯ **Delegate responsibility.** Help your people to think creatively and develop their own unique talents. Whenever possible, let go of the reins and allow your people to perform.

- ✯ **Expect excellence.** If your reps know you think they're capable of reaching greater heights, they'll strive for them.

- ✯ **Remember that recognition is the number one motivator.** Give credibility to your feedback by basing it on the reps' real-world performance. Always have something positive to say, and make it your highest priority every day to give your reps the recognition they deserve.

If you're a manager and you haven't thanked one of your people for doing a good job today, you either have a seriously ill organization on your hands...or you're cheating those people, ripping off assets that they've worked hard to acquire.

—Frank Pacetta

In *Don't Fire Them, Fire Them Up*

Five Goals of a Sales Manager

These five goals are based on feedback from thousands of managers who were asked to list the key criteria for the success of their jobs. Don't hesitate to add more of your own. Then post the list on a large board on your office wall. Each week, set one new goal under each category so that you're constantly coming up with ideas to meet the overall goal, which is to be a great manager. The five major goals of a manager are:

1. **Make quota consistently.** Sales reps are notorious for having their ups and downs. Some months (or weeks) they sell beyond quota, then the following month they get caught up in paperwork and follow-up, and their sales are way down. Help them to reach a consistent level of selling through goal-setting, activity-charting, and rewards and incentives.

2. **Operate at a profit.** With a good sales force, you can sell thousands of items—but the company can go under because the reps are discounting and dropping prices to meet the competition. They do this because they want to get the business. To operate at a profit means to reach the reps value-added selling. When a customer says, "Your price is too high," your reps must know how to tell the customer what he's getting for that additional money. Teach reps to stress the uniqueness

of your product, the personalized attention they offer to the account, and the quality service and follow-up they can expect from your company.

To operate at a profit, it's important to monitor your reps' sales plans, making sure they're realistic and effective. It may mean working with reps on their proposals, and helping them negotiate more effectively. Also, be sure your reps have knowledge of the product line so that they can make informed recommendations to customers. When sales reps are knowledgeable about products and accessories, their ability to find solutions for their customers—solutions that no competitor can offer—is enhanced.

3. **Grow and expand the business.** A good sales manager is constantly feeding the team new ways to get new customers and to branch into new markets. This means monitoring reps' activity levels, both for new reps and for the more experienced.

   One of the biggest problems with experienced reps is that they cut down on prospecting after they have landed one or two prime accounts from which they derive most of their income. However, should they lose one of these accounts, they'll be in real trouble. Not only will the income cease, they'll have forgotten their prospecting skills—unless you motivate them to keep prospecting all the time. Other activities include:

   ☆   Going to trade shows.

   ☆   Asking present customers for referrals.

☆ Developing creative financing for customers so they can afford your products.

☆ Implementing and encouraging networking techniques such as sending congratulations notes to people who have been newly hired, promoted, or received an award; sending announcement cards letting businesses know you've just made a sale or installation to one of their neighbors; sending thank-you notes to people who *don't* buy from you; and most important, by giving 100 percent service and going beyond what customers expect.

4. **Build a strong team.** A manager who can recruit qualified people, motivate, train and coach his team will have no trouble reaching the first three of these goals. There are five levels to building a good team, and a good manager takes equal care and concern with each level:

☆ Select and recruit the best people.

☆ Develop excellent training methods so reps have extensive knowledge of the product, the sales cycle, the customers, and the competition.

☆ Motivate and monitor.

☆ Reward monetarily and emotionally.

☆ Promote with title and/or compensation.

5. **Self-development.** A good manager expects her team to continually build and improve their skills. If you are content to sit on your laurels, you pass that attitude on to your reps. Enthusiasm and excitement about the job, the

product, and the company are contagious. The more you grow and learn, the more you can pass these things on to your team.

Competitive Information Chart

One area in which reps often need help is in answering customer requests for comparisons of your product to your competition's. Reps must be able to focus on your product's unique selling points, and how they compare and contrast to the competition. One way to help them do this is to chart which reps are winning or losing accounts to which competitors, and why. With that knowledge, you can train reps in the value-added selling techniques appropriate to your product and company.

When reps come in from the field, they can go right over to the competitive information chart (whether it's on the wall, in a book, or online) and record the name of the competitor they were selling against, what products they showed, whether they won or lost, and why (price is not always the reason). It may take a few minutes, but it will provide you with invaluable information on your business, your industry, and your area. You may get competitive information guides from the home office, but that won't help you know what your local competitors are doing.

The Competitive Information Chart (see page 56) allows you to collect solid information about your competitors' strengths and weaknesses, as well as your own. Both you and your sales reps can make use of this information. Suppose sales rep A is going against a local competitor on a new account. He can look at the chart and see who has gone against that same competitor lately, and whether they won or lost the sale. If sales rep B won, sales rep A can go to her and say, "How did you get the business?" Perhaps he can get a testimonial from rep B's customer as to why they went with your product. Or if Rep B lost against that competitor, sales rep A can find out why so he doesn't make the same mistakes.

As a manager, you want to examine the chart to determine your most consistent competitor. If reps are constantly losing out to XYZ company, or to XYZ's Super Model #5, you can run a sales meeting devoted specifically on how to sell against that company and that product.

Frank Pacetta, district sales manager of Xerox, and author of *Don't Fire Them, Fire Them Up,* believes that reps must know as much about their competitors' products as they know about their own. He even gives his reps pop quizzes at sales meetings to test their knowledge of the competition. "I'll end a meeting by handing out a six question multiple-choice quiz," he says. "I'm not looking to grade anybody and make a big deal of it, but if the knowledge level is slipping, I'll let the group know that it's time to start boning up on the competition."

Competitive Information Chart

Rep's Name/Date	Your Product/ Model #	Competitor's Product/Model #	Won/Lost	Why?
			W / L	
			W / L	
			W / L	
			W / L	
			W / L	
			W / L	
			W / L	
			W / L	
			W / L	

Creating a Motivating Environment

There are many ways to get people motivated. You can promise them great rewards. You can bribe them. You can fire them up with inspirational messages. You can even yell and scream and threaten them with bodily harm. You might even see results from these methods—for a time. But the true purpose of motivation is not to create short-term bursts of energy. The real purpose is to help people reach beyond what they themselves think they can do, and help them to achieve their very best.

Your job as manager is to combine energy-producing activities, such as premeeting assignments, and contests, with a long-term motivating environment that encourages people to do their best at all times.

A motive is something a person wants or needs. Motivation occurs when people see the connection between specific activities and a chance to satisfy their basic needs. A rep who has a pressing need for money will be motivated knowing that making five demonstrations in a week will get her a $50 bonus. Another rep, who is motivated by pride in achievement, will do better striving to make Rep of the Month. How do you know what motivates people? Here are several categories:

- ✮ Recognition.
- ✮ Money and material goods.
- ✮ Career advancement opportunities.
- ✮ Pride in achievement.
- ✮ An opportunity to give service to others.
- ✮ Relationships with fellow workers.
- ✮ Competition with others.

Notice that recognition is at the top of the list. Studies have shown this to be true over and over again. Mary Kay Ash, the late founder of Mary Kay Cosmetics, had more than 300,000 salespeople in her organization. When doing research for my book *Diamond in the Rough,* I asked Mary Kay how she keeps her people motivated and excited. She replied, "Whenever I meet anybody in the elevator or the hall, I say, 'Hi, how are you?' If I haven't met them before, they'll say, 'Oh, I'm fine, I'm okay.' And I say, 'No, you're *great.* Remember that.' The next time I say, "Hi, how are you?' They say, 'I'm great!' That enthusiasm helps them to feel better about themselves, and it helps me to feel better as well. The result is that everybody goes around here with smiles on their faces and everybody *is* great."

One of the most important lessons Mary Kay ever learned, she said, was to visualize every person you meet as having a sign on their chest that says, "Make me feel important." Do your best to make that happen. Find out what's important to them, ask them questions, and put yourself in their shoes.

There's an old saying that goes, "Our rewards in life are in direct proportion to our service." That's true on an individual level, and on an organizational level as well. The more you value your people, the better they feel about themselves, the more they will be motivated to achieve, and the stronger the foundation for the success of your team and your company will be.

This is not just some feel-good philosophy. There are definite bottom-line advantages:

- ☆ People who are undervalued and unmotivated are dissatisfied, turn in poor performance, and ultimately leave their jobs. Costs of recruiting new employees, especially with high turnover, can skyrocket.

- ☆ People who feel appreciated also feel a sense of pride and ownership, put in greater effort, and consequently increase productivity.

- ☆ Valued and motivated employees maintain better relationships with customers. As Charles McLane, vice president of human resources for Holiday Inn explains, "Well-trained, well-supported, empowered employees provide superior levels of customer service, which encourages the customer to return, which leads to higher revenues, lower operating costs, and higher profits."

Here are some techniques for creating a motivating environment:

✯ **Post your mission statement on the wall.** The team should be able to see its goals at a glance and know what's expected of them.

✯ **Set up a "war room" atmosphere.** Make the physical environment a place where people want to come to work, where they get positive messages, and where they can see their goals set out before them. Use wall space as a gallery for reminders of reps' achievements. Michael Liess, director of the western region of Oce USA, has designated a "top gun" wall, where he posts photos of those who have met activity targets. Remind your reps of the saying, "You become what you think about." Surround them with motivational quotes and educational materials so that they can always be learning and improving their skills.

✯ **Start right at the beginning.** Motivation starts on the very first day a rep is hired. Too often, a rep is hired, goes to personnel to fill out his forms, and is then told, "Go up to the sales department and someone will show you to your desk." It's going to be awfully hard for that rep to feel comfortable in that kind of environment. Jim Miller, CEO of BT Miller Business Systems, believes that the first day on the job is the most important of an employee's career. Knowing that new hires will have butterflies before they start work, he sends a letter of welcome to the person's home the week before their starting date. On their first day of work, reps are given an orientation in the training room and assigned a buddy. That buddy (who is theirs for 30 days) takes them around and introduces them

59

to people in the company. At the end of the day, they get a team shirt. Miller makes sure everyone feels they belong from day one, and gives them immediate recognition for having made the smart decision to join the BT Miller family.

★ **Learn your reps' business and personal goals.** The more you understand about the whole person, the better you'll be able to motivate that individual. Hand your reps a piece of paper. On the top of one side, write, "**Business** Goals for This Year." Write "**Personal Goals** for This Year" on the other side. Have them take it home, and see what they come up with on their own. Not only will this help the reps focus on their own needs and desires, it gives you better insight into the small things you can do on a daily basis to help your reps succeed.

★ **Follow the rules of positive reinforcement.** Behavior that gets rewarded is behavior that gets repeated. If you want someone to behave in a certain way (make more cold calls, pick up more buying signals, for example), then you must reward them for that behavior. Here are some rules to follow to make that process effective:

1. *Give an immediate reward.* It's nice to get an end-of-the-year bonus or praise at a monthly sales meeting, but if the reward is not given soon after the event, it loses its impact. The rep must be able to make an immediate connection between improved performance and getting a reward.

2. *Be as specific as possible.* The rep must be able to identify the behavior for which he's being rewarded. Just saying "You did a good job," is not as effective as saying, "I'm pleased you were able to make 20 more cold calls this week. Your effort is really paying off."

3. *Be consistent and persistent.* You can't reward someone once and expect him to make permanent changes. Keep the rewards going until the behavior becomes habitual to the rep.

4. *Keep praise proportionate to the accomplishment.* If you give too much praise, or your praise is insincere, reps will peg you as a phony and you will lose respect. On the other hand, if the accomplishment is noteworthy and you barely mention it, the person will feel cheated and resistant to repeating the effort.

5. *Use both oral and written praise.* Everyone loves to hear how well they're doing. But it's also nice to get it in writing, so that we can read it over and over again and share it with friends and family. So when a rep has done exceptionally well, you might want to send him a memo to that effect, or even write a personal letter to his home.

Short-term Motivational Activities

Most salespeople are competitive by nature, and will naturally rise to a challenge. If you want to get their energy levels up and increase activity, there's nothing like a contest to get the adrenaline flowing. Sometimes we need to be creative in the activities we use to help our people achieve their goals. Here are some contests and exercises that can help.

The negative comment jar

One of the most destructive forces among sales teams is the negative comment syndrome. One person starts making remarks about low morale, product complaints, or overbearing managers, and negativity spreads like a cancer, blocking everyone's sales success. One way to counter this situation: Every time someone in the office makes a negative comment, they have to put $1 in the jar. If managers make a negative comment, they have to put $5 in the jar. At the end of the month, the top sales rep or the person who made the most cold calls wins the money. Negativity will become a joke, and the atmosphere in the office will definitely improve.

Real-play vs. role-play

Sit your sales team around a table with a phone in the center. Choose a goal, such as having the reps secure appointments over the phone. Have everyone bring in their prospect list, and have each rep put $1 (or one plastic chip) into the pot. The first person who gets an appointment wins the pot. If the rep is unsuccessful, open a discussion about what went right with the call and what could be improved.

This might be a bit nerve-wracking for your team, but your job is to keep a positive atmosphere. Praise everything that goes right with each call, whether or not they get an appointment.

Don't forget to take your turn as well. Let your team know that what you expect of them, you're willing to do as well. Rich Luisi, southeast area vice president of

Electrolux and winner of the Area VP of the Year award two years in a row, says, "the most important element for credibility of a sales manager is to lead by example. That shows everybody you're not asking them to do something you wouldn't do yourself."

Real-play has three important benefits:

1. It gives you an opportunity to spend time with your people and give positive feedback on what went right with the call and what can be improved.

2. All the reps get to hear and pick up ideas from their peers.

3. In surveys of more than 10,000 sales managers, lack of prospecting activity came up as the number one deficiency with their salespeople. So while your reps are training during this action plan, they're actually generating activity and producing income at the same time.

Premeeting assignments

At each sales meeting, ask one or two of your most experienced reps to make a 15-minute presentation in the next meeting on topics in which they're exceptionally skilled (such as closing, networking, or demonstrating). Or assign a presentation to a rep who is deficient in a specific area. Give her a minimum of two weeks to prepare. In most cases, because the rep wants to look good in front of her peers, she prepares so thoroughly she becomes proficient in that area.

This not only helps the rep retain information she's researched (remember the rule: Hear and you forget, see and you remember, do and you understand), it also helps you to evaluate the rep's understanding of that particular skill. When the rep does an excellent presentation (which she usually does because of the preparation involved), it's a perfect time to recognize and praise her efforts in front of the group.

Win-win contests

Some contests have one winner; often the same person wins time and again. Don Duncan, president of Val-Pak of Southeast Michigan and number one in the country for mailing volume, has come up with a scenario that allows several people to "win" each month. "We've identified five components of what it takes to be a top Val-Pak salesperson," he says. "Gross billing, number of clients handled, number of new clients, percentage of money collected, and average sale price. Every month, we acknowledge the top people in each particular category. We had one salesperson, a marginal producer, who one month was top in collecting her money up front. When she saw her name in writing, we began to get more activity from her and now she's doing really well."

Winning in one area enabled that rep to do well in others. Devising a contest where several people win allows you to spread the recognition around, thereby building your team's overall confidence and performance.

One problem equals two solutions

Managers spend a lot of time trying to put out fires. If you're running around trying to solve one problem after another, you create the impression you're out of control. You can eliminate 50 percent of the fires by asking a rep who comes to you with a problem, "What do you think you should do?" Let your reps know that your door is always open to them, but that you also recognize their own problem-solving abilities. Often, the rep will come up with the best answer, to which you might say, "Excellent idea, Paula. Go ahead and do that."

One manager I know in Chicago has a sign on her door that reads, "One problem, two solutions, please." When someone comes to her with a problem, they must offer two solutions, no matter how crazy those solutions seem. This ensures that the reps learn to think on their own. Coming to the manager to solve their problems can be habit-forming for reps, especially new hires. When you get your reps to come up with their own solutions and praise them for their efforts, you get them in the habit of thinking for themselves. This not only shows that you trust their judgment, it lets them know you think they're capable of much more than they might realize themselves.

The dart contest

This contest is designed according to the type of sales in which your company is involved. For instance, you may award reps one dart for every Model A Widget they sell, two darts for every Model B, and so on. Or you may want to reward activity, not just sales results, by awarding a certain number of darts for every 10 or 20 cold calls they make. You then mark prizes on small pieces of paper (one might be marked "$10," another, "a pen and pencil set," "$100," "a pocket calculator," for example), stick them into balloons, blow up the balloons, and paste them onto a dartboard or large wooden plank. Then each rep gets to throw his or her darts. They don't know which prize is in which balloon. So that means that reps with the most darts get more turns, but everyone has an equal chance at winning the bigger prizes. The key about this contest is that you're rewarding reps on the motivation factors: You're giving them recognition because the ones who are more successful have more darts, and you're making it competitive,by having money and prizes at stake.

Telemarketing teams

Suppose you have six reps on your team. You break them up into two teams. Monday morning at 8:30, have all six reps get on the phone and keep going until noon. They break for lunch and begin again. The teams get points according to the number of calls they make, appointments they get, or demonstrations they set up. As the manager, you play sports announcer during the day, announcing which individuals and which teams are taking the lead. The reason for the split into teams is that if there is one person who is continually leading, others may simply give up, thinking that they have no chance to catch up. But when teams compete, reps encourage each other to try harder. It's not only a competitive game, it's also a way to build team camaraderie.

Suit me fine

In this contest, the prize for the winning rep is a business suit. If you go to a local store, you can usually negotiate a discounted rate for buying six or 12 suits during the year. The winning rep can present a voucher to the store for his or her suit. This prize kills two birds with one stone. It helps your reps look their best, while rewarding them for meeting and/or exceeding goals.

The blitz

Salespeople are often out on their own, facing a lot of rejection. For a change of pace, you might arrange a blitz day. When Mike Liess of Oce USA wants to generate activity quickly, he conducts a "mega-blitz." Liess explains, "We bring in managers and support people from other divisions and line up every salesperson with one of these people. Then we go out on a day-long prospecting blitz. We wrap up at 6 p.m. and talk about the day. Then we hold a drawing for those who've gotten at least four qualified prospects. We hope that the results will encourage the reps to go out and blitz the next day on their own."

You can add a kick to this activity by designating a few accounts as "blue dots." The reps don't know which accounts are blue dots, but if they come back with information, an appointment, or a sale from that company, they win a special prize. This encourages everyone to make as many calls as possible because they never know which one may be the secret account.

Making Quota *Through* Your Reps, Not *For* Them

There are probably more than a few salespeople who have been slightly embarrassed at one time or another by a sales manager who could not wait for the right things to happen during a presentation. Rather than risk losing the sale, the sales manager took over and closed the deal. That may be good for sales and quota, but it is never the right way to train salespeople. Here are some hints on how to handle letting reps succeed on their own:

Are you willing to let go?

Do you want to know what category of manager you fall into? Ask yourself these questions:

- ☆ How often do you find yourself taking over calls for your sales reps?
- ☆ Why can't your sales reps perform these activities on their own?
- ☆ How do you know your reps are unable to perform these functions?
- ☆ Why don't you let your reps make mistakes?
- ☆ What do you think they'd learn from their mistakes?

★ What do you think their mistakes might teach you?

★ What message does it send to your reps when you jump in all the time?

It's instinctive for a manager to want to jump in and save a sale, but the message you're sending is that you don't trust your rep. Then, when the rep is on her own, she'll have no experience in handling tough situations herself.

Start with small accounts

Nobody wants to lose a sale. And if you're on a really important call and the rep is making a serious error, then you're right to step in. There are often smaller situations where you can let the rep stand or fall on his own. All he's doing is generating leads; the manager always comes in for the close. Reps get burnt-out from going out on calls and never being able to complete the entire sales cycle.

Realize that one mistake does not necessarily mean a lost sale

Just because the rep has made an error or missed a cue doesn't always mean the sale is gone. Often, the customer feels empathy for a rep who is trying hard and making an effort. Or the customer may not even notice a mistake that seems glaring to you. And some customers even get upset when the manager is constantly cutting the rep off midstream.

Close a deal for a rep and you've made one sale; teach him how to close and you've made a career.

Be a leader, not a manipulator. It's amazing what we sometimes do to manipulate other people. Often we're not even aware of what we're doing. What we want to do is help other people, and what we end up doing is alienating them.

The Sales Manager's Role Checklist

If you want your reps to succeed, you must let them know that you respect and admire their ability. You want the rep to become your partner, not your adversary. When something is very important to you—whether it's meeting your quota or bringing in that big account—when you want to make sure it comes out well, it's only natural to want to retain control of the situation. But there are times, when in order to lead well, you have to let go of the reins. When that happens, those around you feel as though you care about them. They will want to prove to you that you were right to place your faith in them, and they, too, will want the best possible results.

"I start with the premise that the function of leadership is to produce more leaders, not more followers."

—Ralph Nader, consumer advocate

☑ **Paste these goals where you can see them every day. Each week set one new goal under each category.**

1. Make quota consistently.
2. Operate at a profit.
3. Grow and expand the business.
4. Build a strong team.
5. Encourage self-development.

☑ **Competitive Information Chart.** Use the Competitive Information Chart (see page 56) to help reps answer customers' concerns about your product or service in comparison to your competitor's.

☑ **Create a motivating environment.** All sales reps are not alike. Some will be motivated by money, and some by a need for recognition. Others may be looking for a promotion into management. The manager's job is to learn each rep's underlying motive and create an atmosphere that will bring out the best in the individual and in the team. Here are some techniques for creating a motivating environment:

1. Post your mission statement on the wall.
2. Set a "war room" atmosphere.
3. Start motivating right from the very first day.
4. Learn your reps' business and personal goals.
5. Follow the rules of positive reinforcement:

   ☆ Give an immediate reward.

   ☆ Be as specific as possible.

   ☆ Be consistent and persistent.

   ☆ Keep praise proportionate to accomplishment.

   ☆ Use both oral and written praise.

6. Create motivating contests and exercises (see pages 61-67).

☑ **Make quota *through* your reps, not *for* them.** Are you giving your reps the opportunities they need to succeed on their own? Or do you always jump in and close at the first sign of trouble? Here are some hints on how to let go of that tendency:

1. Ask yourself how often you take over calls for your reps, why your reps can't perform on their own, what you think they'd learn from their mistakes, what you might learn, and what message it sends to your reps when you jump in all the time.

70

2. Start with small accounts where there is not
    so much at stake.

Realize that if a rep makes one mistake, it doesn't necessarily mean the sale is lost.

CHAPTER 4

SALES REP PERFORMANCE EVALUATION

A sales manager must have a keen eye and a good memory. It's part of your job description to be able to look at a rep's performance, judge his strengths and weaknesses, and determine whether his sales performance is improving. A keen eye and a good memory can be aided by setting up effective systems of evaluation and proper ways of documenting your observations. Documenting performance does more than just keep you out of trouble should you be facing a lawsuit. It helps you focus on specific areas that need improvement, and it helps you remember them from one evaluation to the next so that you have something to measure against.

You Can't Expect
What You Don't Inspect

Your job is to build the best team possible. That means you have to monitor each individual on the team to be sure he is living up to his potential. Here are some techniques and guidelines to help you evaluate your reps' performance.

Three key guidelines for performance evaluation

Performance evaluation does not mean performance criticism. It is an opportunity for you and your reps to come to an agreement about ways in which they can combat their deficiencies. The three key guidelines for performance evaluation are:

1. **Be specific, detailed, and objective.** Telling a rep she "did not pick up on a customer's buying signals" is not going to be effective if the rep doesn't know exactly what you mean. Be specific, detailed, and objective. Fill in these blanks:

Date of call: _____

Name of customer: _____

_____

Summary of conversation: _____

_____

_____

_____

Use the Coaching Form in Chapter 6 to help keep accurate records. That way, your feedback will be based on facts. When all these facts have been laid out, the rep will know exactly what she did wrong, and how she can improve. This also makes it possible for you to review the call later if necessary.

2. **Feedback must be timely.** The best time to give feedback is right after a call, or by the end of the day. You want to go over events while they're still fresh in the rep's mind. This is true in any field, not just in sales, as was demonstrated once when I went to see heavyweight contender Shannon Briggs fight. Briggs hadn't lost a fight yet, it was his birthday, and he wanted a knockout. But his opponent wouldn't give in. Briggs finally won by decision, but he was clearly frustrated. Although friends and fans (myself included) were waiting to congratulate Briggs, and reporters were hustling for an interview, trainer Teddy Atlas took Briggs aside right after the fight and asked him, "What do you think went on in there? What could you have done differently? What did you learn from this fight?" He then gave Briggs insight into what went right, and what went wrong. He was evaluating the performance while the event was still fresh.

   This is the kind of feedback Briggs would remember going into his next fight. The same goes for your reps: Don't wait until next week or until the next performance review to let the reps know how they're doing. Keep evaluations timely and they'll go into the next call with your advice fresh in mind.

3. **Never overwhelm.** Here's another sports analogy: I once went to a golf pro for some lessons. On the driving range he kept telling me, "Hold your hands like this, bend your knees this way, put your arms down, look at the ball." He gave me so many instructions, I could barely hit the ball. I was a better golfer

before I took lessons. Don't overwhelm reps with too much information at once. Choose one or two priority areas that need improvement. But be sure to include positive evaluations as well, and end the session with an area in which the rep has made a visible effort to improve.

Measuring Reps' Activity Levels

Ask a group of managers for the single most important reason reps fail to achieve, and they'll tell you "lack of activity." In every industry, the biggest complaint is that reps are not prospecting enough. That's why activity reports were invented.

Today, sales managers are exposed to countless methods of measuring and monitoring their sales teams' activities. Paper and computerized forms such as 3-day account forecasts, cold call sheets, presentation and demonstration reports, and so many other systems help managers keep track of their sales reps' prospecting and accounting information. Although these report forms are important, sales managers are often overwhelmed with the paperwork and spend more time managing paper than they do people.

Perhaps you have your reps keep a daily log of their calls and appointments. You might ask them for a 30-60-90-day forecast of who they've called on, how much dollar potential is involved, what's the percentage of closing the deal, and when they expect to close it. In reality, this is a wish list. You often get the same list handed in every month with one or two changes.

Sometimes these reports become mere exercises—paperwork that no one ever reads. There's a story one rep tells about how when asked for his usual 30-day forecast he handed in a sheet that read, "sunny, windy, rain, sunny, rain, windy..." Every month for three months he handed in his 30-day weather forecast and got no response. The manager wasn't even looking at the reports!

Of course, there are many reports that work well and serve a useful purpose. If you are not sure whether your reports are having the effect you want—which is to accurately measure activity levels—ask these four questions to outline what the benefits and drawbacks are:

1. What kind of forms or programs are you currently using to monitor your sales reps activity levels?

2. What are some of the benefits of such reports to you and your sales reps?

3. What are some of the drawbacks of such reports to you and your sales reps?

4. What if some of these reports could be eliminated? How much more time could you spend with your people?

Going by the MAP

There are two major problems with monitoring activity levels. First, there are many stages involved in every sale, and activity reports don't always tell you where the sale is stalling, or why.

Second, a sales manager can't be everywhere with everyone at once. A good manager will go out into the field with his reps and evaluate on-the-job performance. But when you're out in the field, how do you keep track of all your other reps' work? What if you were able to set up a system that could allow you to immediately evaluate and understand reps' lack of activity, or why they're being blocked from moving along in the sales cycle?

What I'm suggesting is not exactly a high-tech solution (see Chapter 5 for more about technology). There's nothing wrong with using technology, but there's definitely something to be said for the war room concept—keeping visual reminders posted that keep people on track and moving forward. You can't depend on technology to meet all your needs.

I saw this for myself when I attended a production meeting with one of the most successful manufacturing companies in the country. On one wall they hung a huge whiteboard with magnetic pieces that they move around based upon various projects and their stages of development. When they have production meetings, everyone can clearly see the pieces on the board, discuss them, and move them around if necessary. This multi-million dollar company has found this simple system more effective for visualizing the progress of its many projects than any technology that has come out so far.

One valuable tool you can use in your office is a MAP (Management Account Profile) board—a practical visual aid to help you focus on your teams' activity and receive immediate feedback on how sales reps are managing and growing territories.

Using the MAP board, you can walk around the office and, within three minutes, evaluate each sales rep's performance in each of the stages of the sales cycle. You'll be able to tell when people are not making enough calls, when proposals are being sent out and not followed through, and when the cycle stalls in the closing stages. Anybody can tell a sales rep to "get more numbers." The MAP board allows you to evaluate each person's performance strengths and deficiencies, and then strategize with them to help them move their accounts from one stage to another in a timely fashion. Here's how it works:

Each salesperson has his or her own 2 x 3-foot cork-board, a set of map tacks or pushpins, and 30 to 40 small blank cards. Across the top of the corkboard are headings that represent each stage of your company's typical sales cycle. For example, First Call, Presentation, Demonstration, Proposal, and Close. Your stages might be different, depending on the type of business.

Let's say a sales rep goes out on a first call. After qualifying the account, the sales rep comes back to the office and fills out an account card using the following information:

1. Name of the company.
2. Date of the call.
3. Product and/or dollar potential (if applicable).

Once the card is filled out, it is then posted on the MAP under the First Call column. As each stage of the sale is completed, the account cards will move across the MAP until they end up in the closing stage. The MAP board focuses on key priorities; allows your reps to see how they're doing, where they've been, and where they're going; and helps you coach them more immediately, actively, and effectively.

Sample Account Card

Account Name:_____		
Stage Completed	Date	Product
____ Stage 1	————	
____ Stage 1	————	XXXXX
____ Stage 1	————	
____ Stage 1	————	$ Potential
____ Stage 1	————	$15K

Sample MAP Boards: Week 1

First Call	2nd Stage Presentation	3rd Stage Demo	4th Stage Proposal	5th Stage Close
A	H	J		
B	I			
C				
D				
E				
F				
G				

Week 1 in a 30–45 day sales cycle. Three accounts have already been moved to the second and third stages. The first stage has room for more cards because this is where most of the activity will be generated.

Sample MAP Boards: Week 2

First Call		2nd Stage Presentation	3rd Stage Demo	4th Stage Proposal	5th Stage Close
A	M	C	H	J	
B	N	I			
E	O	D			
F	P				
G					
K					
L					

Here we see that the sales rep has generated six more new accounts in the first stage and moved C,D,H,J accounts across the MAP.

Sample MAP Boards: Week 8

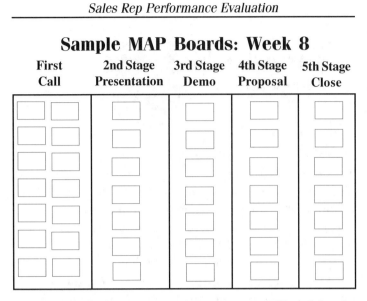

First Call	2nd Stage Presentation	3rd Stage Demo	4th Stage Proposal	5th Stage Close

Jumping ahead to week eight, we see all the stages filled with activity, representing a highly productive sales representative in action. Note that the first stage should always have twice as many accounts as the others.

MAP Board Checklist

☑ **Be proactive, not reactive.** Coach sales reps on a weekly basis according to where they are at every stage. You can look at the board and see right where the activity is centered: There may be a lot of initial activity in Stage 1 and no presentations scheduled; there might be several proposals in Stage 4 and no closings. Your job is to evaluate performance deficiencies immediately.

☑ **Make sure you're using positive recognition.** Recognition is the salesperson's most powerful motivator. If sales reps are having problems closing, but they're generating a lot of initial sales activity, be sure to reinforce the positive before moving on to evaluate closing problems.

☑ **Sell your reps on the value of the MAP board.** Make sure the reps understand its value and benefits. You don't want to force them to follow a program they don't understand. If they don't buy into its value, they won't use it. Share your enthusiasm for the system and it will work for everyone. Sell your reps on its value the way you would sell any product: through the questioning process. "What are the stages of our sales cycle? What if I could give you a system that showed you every area of the sales cycle and what accounts were in each stage at any given time—something that could eliminate a major portion of the paperwork you now do. Would that be of benefit to you?"

☑ **Date each account card.** You can see how long each card has been posted, and you can formulate time limits. For instance, you can say that if a card hasn't moved in four or six weeks, it must be removed from the board.

You don't want boards filled with outdated and obsolete accounts.

☑ **Post monthly and/or yearly goals next to the board.** Both you and your sales staff can easily see the relationship between their goals and the specific, detailed activity posted on the board.

☑ **Encourage friendly competition.** One of the benefits of the board is that it is in plain view. Salespeople can then compare notes, see who has the most activity, and emulate the best reps' boards.

Evaluating the Team

It is just as important to evaluate your team as it is to evaluate individual reps. When you gather information from each of your reps, you must look at it from two points of view: first, as an indicator of how that rep is performing; and second, as a means of comparison with other reps' performance. Here are some techniques you can use for spotting team deficiencies.

In-field observation

As you go out into the field with your sales reps, take notes on how they build rapport, how they ask questions, how they qualify, how they present, and how they close (see Coaching Form in Chapter 6). The notes that you take are then used to evaluate and coach the individual rep.

But when you travel with several reps, you may begin to see a pattern of deficiencies. If many of your reps are having difficulty closing, for example, you would know that this is a necessary topic for a future sales meeting. You can utilize the input you get from traveling with your reps to customize meetings around critical areas.

Follow-up letters

Many managers find it helpful to require reps to send their customers follow-up letters after each appointment, outlining what was discussed in the meeting and what the next step will be. Ask your reps for copies of these letters, and read through them. You can learn a lot about how your reps are conducting sales calls, and how well they're tuning into customer needs. These letters may also give you an indication of common weaknesses amongst the team, which could be addressed in a sales meeting or training session.

Account follow-up

If a rep loses an account, you can get feedback on his or her performance by calling the customer to say, "This is John Smith, manager of ABC Corporation. I just wanted to call and thank you for the time you spent with Sally Green, our sales representative. I understand that you've gone with another vendor, but I was wondering if you could give me some feedback. It would be very valuable for us to know why you chose not to go with us. Was it the product? Was it the salesperson?"

The information you get might, once again, point out a pattern of areas where reps need improvement. There have been occasions where this kind of follow-up call has saved the account as well.

If the sale was successful, you might want to call and say, "This is John Smith, manager of ABC Corporation. I know that Sally Green is taking care of you, but as a manger, I like to call my reps' new accounts to thank them for the business and find out if there's any way I can be of service. I also wondered if I might get some feedback from you. What made you choose our company? Was it the product? Was it the salesperson?"

It makes customers feel special when someone calls and thanks them for their business. And the positive feedback allows you to find out what your reps are doing well, and reinforce their performance strengths.

Performance Evaluation Checklist

☑ **Be specific, detailed, and objective.** Let your reps know exactly what they've done wrong so they know where to focus their efforts.

☑ **Feedback must be timely.** The best time to give feedback is immediately following the event, or at least by the end of the day.

☑ **Never overwhelm.** Focus on one or two priority deficiencies.

☑ **Measure reps' activity levels.** Are you managing paperwork instead of people? If your reports are not having the desired effect (which is to measure, monitor, and improve the sales reps' activity in the field), answer these three questions:

☆ What kinds of forms are you currently using to monitor your sales reps' activity levels?

☆ What are some of the benefits to you and your sales reps?

☆ What are some of the drawbacks to you and your sales reps?

☑ **Going by the MAP.** Use the Management Account Profile board as a practical visual aid to help you focus on your team's activity levels. The MAP board will show exactly which accounts are in which stages of the sales cycle, and let you know in which areas your reps may need coaching.

Here are some techniques for using the MAP board to its full advantage:

☆ Be proactive, not reactive.

☆ Make sure you're using positive recognition.

☆ Sell your reps on the value of the MAP board.

☆ Date each account card.

☆ Post monthly or yearly goals next to the board.

☆ Encourage friendly competition.

☑ **Evaluating the team.** Comparing your reps' performance in various areas can give you a good indication of your team's overall strengths and weaknesses. Here are three ways you can use reps' evaluations to measure your team's performance:

1. In-field observation.
2. Follow-up letters.
3. Account follow-up.

CHAPTER 5

TIME
MANAGEMENT
AND
TECHNOLOGY

To many people, time management means segmenting their lives (especially their work lives) into little boxes, with each box representing a certain number of minutes or hours. To me, time management means putting things in perspective. Think about the 4.5 billion years Earth has been in existence. Think about the 70-plus years the average person spends on Earth. Put into that perspective, we are here on Earth for the blink of an eye. We have much to accomplish in such a brief time.

Time management is learning to appreciate the value of every moment you have on Earth. Not every moment will be earth-shattering. There will be moments of excitement, moments of success, moments of failure, and moments of introspection. But no moment should go to waste. You can't plan every moment of your life (or your reps' lives), but you can look at how you and your team spend your moments and think about whether or not you are spending your time wisely—and if not, find ways to make necessary changes.

The Time Management Test

There's an old saying that goes, "It's not how hard you work, it's how smart you work." Although we'd like to think otherwise, hard work alone doesn't guarantee success. There are many people who work hard all their lives and don't achieve success. Working smart is the ability to make sure that while you work hard, you use the most productive means possible to get the job accomplished. It's the ability to do a task, evaluate it, and see how that task can be done better the next time. It's discovering how you can become more efficient each time you do something. It's understanding what your strengths are, and building on them. It's learning from every action you take and converting that knowledge into the ability to make a better decision the next time.

The best way for your reps to work smarter is to manage their time so that they know what kinds of tasks they have to accomplish, and the best times to accomplish them. That often means dividing their time into face-to-face (or voice-to-voice) sales time, and non-selling activity time.

There's an exercise I use in my sales management training seminar, designed for managers to give to their whole team, called the "Time Management Test." It's really very simple. Give your reps these directions: Starting on Monday, keep a journal of what you're doing every hour that you're working. If you start at 9:00, stop work at 9:55 and record what your last hour's activity has been. Do the same thing at the end of each hour throughout the day. On Friday, compare that week's activity and productivity to the week before.

I guarantee your reps will have accomplished more during their journal-keeping week than they ever have before.

Why? Because they had to think about everything they

did. They were forced to think about the hour they just spent and how they could have improved it, and the hour to come and how they were going to spend it. It's proactive thinking about how they can work more efficiently, whether that means increasing their time in front of customers or on the phone, changing the time of day during which they do paperwork, or changing their driving route so that they spend less time on the road. Your reps automatically start allocating their time more wisely.

This test is all about the ability to look at the big picture and take the time to think about what you can do to work smarter. Sometimes that's all it takes—not making giant changes, but taking the time to think about what you're doing and what small changes you can make to improve your overall efficiency.

> *"You will never find time for anything. If you want time, you must make it."*
>
> —Charles Buxton, statesman

Five Best Ways to Manage Your Time (and Your Reps' Time)

1. **Emphasize balance.** Obviously, your job is to keep everyone efficient and productive at work. Just remember that work is not everything. When the pressure at work is at its worst, people tend to neglect other areas of life that are equally important. For yourself and for your team, keep that perspective in mind. Balance your time among work, family, and personal interests. Urge your reps to make a list of the top 10 things they want to do in the next 12 months—not just work goals, but personal goals as well—and to look

at it at least once a week to check their progress.

2. **Get out from under your e-mail.** E-mail has its good points, but it can be overwhelming. It's easy to feel that we are at the mercy of our email—that we have to pay attention to it at all times. People will call and say, "Did you get the e-mail I sent you 15 minutes ago?" The solution is to think of your e-mail as being delivered like your paper mail, and that you will only check it at a specific time. The idea that you must send an instant response is damaging to productivity.

3. **Rearrange your environment.** Are you convinced you are managing time well because you're doing things the way they've always been done? It may be that you are just taking the easy way out. You don't have to make major changes to be more efficient, just make minor adjustments. Simply moving a file cabinet, changing your filing system, or moving your desk to a new position may make a huge difference. Look at your reps' spaces and think about ways you might change their environment. And if it doesn't work out, you can always put things back the way they were.

4. Concentrate on one thing at a time. David Allen, a business expert, once said, "You can do anything, but you can't do everything." What I take that to mean is that you can do it all, but you can't do it all at the same time. You have to acknowledge that you are a human being with human limitations. You have to take everything in sequence. Write down the sequence and say, "I'll do this task first,

it should take me this long. Then I'll do the next one." Otherwise, it's like gridlock with everybody trying to cross the intersection at the same time. No one goes anywhere. This applies not only to business, but to life in general. It's all about setting up a sequence of priorities. It's common sense, but it's difficult to think about when you're caught in the fray. That's why you need to make it a habit in your life.

5. **Customize your time management method.** There are many useful time management tools and programs on the market today. One of them may work perfectly for you, but none of them work perfectly for everyone. Find one— or create one yourself—that is best suited for you as an individual. Every high achiever I've met has an individual system that he or she has devised to help manage time. Some are complicated, and some are as simple as a little black book. The system you use is less important than using a system that works for you.

"I am definitely going to take a course on time management...just as soon as I can work it into my schedule."

—Louis Boone, editor

The Marriage of Sales and Technology

One of the biggest changes in the past few years has been the introduction of computer technology into the selling process. Contact management, sales force automation, and customer relationship management software programs such as ACT, Goldmine, and Sales Logix have made many salespeople's lives much easier. There is no particular program that is the best across the board; it takes time and research to determine which one will work most efficiently for your company. However, no matter how good the program, it will only be effective if it fits your company's needs, and is used properly and consistently by your sales force.

But as Debbie Qaqish, vice president of sales and marketing for First Wave Technologies, Inc., explains, "I first started working with computerized sales programs in the early 1990s. At that time there was a huge failure rate when companies tried to adopt technology to help their sales organizations. I left my job and went into a different field for several years. When I decided to return to the field and work for First Wave, I called an old friend and asked him how things had changed in the time I'd been away. He said, 'Nothing is different. People still don't know how to introduce technology into the sales force.' And I've found that to be true because managers don't always understand what technology can and cannot do for them. They don't think about how it's actually going to be used in the field, and they expect that it will solve all their problems. Technology can help your people do their jobs better, but it won't do it for them."

Here are some tips and guidelines to help you understand how to use technology to its greatest advantage:

✩ **Understand a day in the life of a salesperson.**
One of the main reasons technology systems fail to do what they're supposed to do is that they are purchased by the people "upstairs" who don't fully understand the day-to-day processes their salespeople follow. "From a broad perspective," says Qaqish, "software companies are pushing software. Companies are hoping to buy solutions. What's being dropped

out of the middle is the end user and how he'll actually use the program." If you haven't been out in the field with your reps in a while, spend more time with them before you spend time choosing a system.

☆ **Identify the top three frustrations your sales-people consistently experience.** Look for software that can address these problems. If, for instance, your company has a large number of products to offer and customers who need immediate delivery on many items, you would look for software that could help salespeople track inventory numbers so that they could give customers exact availability and delivery information.

☆ **Create an internal marketing campaign to introduce the technology to your sales force.** Change is difficult for everyone. You want to make this transition as easy as possible for everyone who is going to use the new technology you're introducing. In most companies, there will be some people who can't wait to embrace the new system, while others will be kicking and screaming against it the whole time. Salespeople often feel that technology is being forced down their throats while their "old" systems work perfectly well. If you have mapped out their day-to-day processes, and understand their greatest frustrations, you will be able to explain up front exactly how the new technology will make their lives easier. Don't assume that they will understand the benefits on their own.

☆ **Update the MAP board.** While I still like the idea of a MAP board posted on the wall where everyone can see it, technology can make it easier for the individual salesperson to have his or her own MAP board readily available for changes and updates. The same five stages of the sales cycle (or however many your process includes) can be mapped out on the computer (First Call, Presentation, Demonstration, Proposal, and Close). You could then set up a program so that when information is entered into each phase, a set of questions pops up that can help the salesperson qualify the prospect to move on to the next stage. This could be especially helpful to new reps, who would not only have a visual representation of where they are in the sales process, but also have an immediate training aid to be sure they're proceeding logically and effectively through the sales cycle.

★ **Don't get carried away by what you think technology can do.** Qaqish tells the story of one company that came to her looking for customer relationship management software. They were excited about all the things this new technology would allow them to do. "Then we started asking them questions," says Qaqish. "When I asked where their salespeople worked, they answered, 'Mostly from home.' So then I asked, 'What kind of Internet connections do they have?' 'Oh,' they said, 'most of them have dial-up connections—and a lot of them have older computers and one phone line.' We had to tell this company that because they weren't willing to buy new equipment or pay for DSL lines for their people, they couldn't expect the kind of results they

94

wanted from technology." Technology is not a magic pill. It's not the cure for all of your company's ills. It has to be considered in a realistic light that includes what kind of equipment your company currently uses and if it can support the new technology you want to use.

☆ **Don't rely on technology rather than relationships.** Used correctly, technology can be a great boon to the sales process. Used incorrectly, it can turn customers away. Don't get me wrong. I use technology. I appreciate the ability to send and receive e-mail anytime and anywhere. Technology is a great tool—it can *help* you close business, but it doesn't do it for you. If it did, all those dot-coms wouldn't have turned into "dot-bombs." Sales are made from relationships, and it's difficult to establish relationships on a computer screen. Keep your e-mails short and to the point, especially because so many people today are reading these messages on PDA's with tiny screens. Technology should help create a more intimate, not a less intimate, relationship with your customers. It can help your salespeople understand more about your clients' business, and help serve customers in a more timely fashion, but it can never take the place of the face-to-face (or even voice-to-voice) meeting, or establish personal relationships. Often, the one thing that gets you past barriers and through objections is the relationship that is formed between the salesperson and the customer. That's why most successful people in this business don't spend their time searching for easy answers or relying on computer software to make the sale. They spend much of their time learning, practicing, and honing their sales techniques, but they spend most of their time building relationships with their customers.

Time Management and Technology Checklist

Five Best Ways to Manage Your Time (and your reps' time).

- ☑ Emphasize balance between work and personal life.

- ☑ Get out from under your e-mail. Don't get caught in the trap of checking it every five minutes. Create specific times to reply and send.

- ☑ Rearrange your environment. Change is good; a change in environment can often spur a change in thinking.

- ☑ Concentrate on one thing at a time. We all have to learn to multitask, but always focus on the task at hand.

- ☑ Customize your time management method. Find the tools and methods (or create them yourself) that are best suited for you as an individual.

☑ **Use technology to its greatest advantage.**

☆ Understand a day in the life of a salesperson. Keep the end-user in mind when deciding which software will work for your team or company.

☆ Identify the top three frustrations your sales-people consistently experience. Look for software that can address these problems.

☆ Create an internal marketing campaign to introduce the technology to your sales force. Make the transition as easy as possible for everyone who is going to use the new technology you're introducing.

☆ Update the MAP board. Set up programs that help your salespeople keep track of where they are in the sales cycle.

☆ Don't get carried away by what you think technology can do. Consider what you want technology to achieve within the parameters of the kind of equipment your company currently uses and if it can support the new technology you want to use.

☆ Don't rely on technology rather than relationships. Technology can help you close business, but it can't close it for you. Remember that a good relationship is the foundation on which the entire sale is built.

CHAPTER 6

SALES REP PERFORMANCE IMPROVEMENT

One of the first things you learn as a sales manager is that no two reps are alike. As a manager, you're going to be dealing with all types of people. You'll be dealing with reps who have no previous sales experience, and reps who've been around for years. You'll be dealing with people of different backgrounds, education levels, personalities, work habits, and personal and professional goals. But one thing they all have in common is room for improvement.

Being a manager can be very frustrating. It's like being a boxing trainer. You can teach your boxer all the right moves, give him guidance, and be right there with him in his corner. Your job is to make him a better fighter, but you can't throw the punches for him. Your job as a manager is to make your team, individually and collectively, the best it can be. The best way to get the best out of your people is through coaching and counseling: to work with them out in the field, to observe their behavior, to reinforce what they do well, and help them improve when they don't do well. Here are some techniques to help you help your reps reach their greatest potential:

Coaching vs. Counseling

Coaching is done on an ongoing basis, and is emphasized when you recognize a particular deficiency.

Counseling is done when the deficiency is not corrected—either because the coaching is ineffective, there is a lack of skill involved, or there are personal or professional problems blocking improvement in a particular area.

As a manager, your main goal is to improve your reps' performance and build a strong team. Sometimes, managers who have been promoted because of their great success in sales miss the thrill of the close. However, with your guidance, coaching, and training, your sales reps can grow, improve, and achieve their own great success. Then you get your greatest reward: No rep ever forgets that special manager who made a difference in their career, and in their life.

Coaching in the Field—Before, During, and After the Sales Call

No matter how many sales forecasts you get from your reps, and how much in-house training and role-playing you provide, the only way to get a true reading of a sales rep's progress is to take a reality check—out in the field, in real-life account call situations where you can get an "up close and personal" view and make accurate evaluations of your rep's strengths and deficiencies.

Before the call

Find out from your reps as much as you can about the account so that: 1) you're both totally prepared for the call; and 2) you can point out to the rep areas where he or she is missing information.

Ask your rep questions before you go out on the call. Questions you might want to ask include:

★ *Who are we seeing on this call?*

★ *Is this the decision-maker?*

★ *What makes you think this person can make the decision today?*

★ *Have you seen anyone else in the organization?*

★ *What can you tell me about the company and its products?*

★ *What makes you think there's a need for our product or service?*

★ *What do you want the customer to do when this call is over?*

★ *Why do you think this customer will take that action? What are the benefits to him?*

★ *What objections do you think he might have to taking that action?*

★ *What's our main goal on this call?*

The last question is the most crucial one to ask. Jorja Coulter, manager of private transfer sales development at Allied Van Lines, calls this "expectation management." She says, "You need to talk with your reps about what their expectations of the call are, what their expectations of *your* role in the call are, and what the customer's expectations of this call may be. The call is successful when everyone's expectations are met."

★ **Be sure the rep remains focused on his objective.** "Many times reps want to change the objective of the call when they know the manager is observing," says Coulter. "They push a little too hard or rely on you a little too much. Be very careful not to let the objective of the call change just because there's another player."

✮ **Be sure the rep has a reason to call on this customer.** Larry Stein, president and general sales manager of Whalen/Weavers Allied Van Lines, is head of a team that includes the two top salespeople in the country—the first time in Allied history that two salespeople from the same agency have won that honor. Stein agrees with Coulter's philosophy. "The biggest mistake you can make is not having a reason to make a call," he says. Many times, when a manager tells a rep he'll be going out on calls with him, the rep takes him to see all his best customers to make a good impression. "That is not a training environment," says Stein. "You have no objective against which to measure the success of the call."

✮ **Stress value-added selling.** Another important question to ask your rep is: What can we do to bring some added value to this customer? "Why would some guy buy our service," asks Stein, "which is a truck going down a road, unless we can provide some value-added?" The idea is to get the rep focused on this customer's key needs, and on what he can offer to best meet those needs.

✮ **Ask your rep, "Is there anything else I should know?"** This is to double-check that you're both on the right track and clear about your goals. There's nothing more unprofessional than a Laurel and Hardy sales rep and manager stumbling over each other because of a lack of preparation and miscommunication.

During the call

One key expectation to discuss with your rep before the call is, "What role do you want me to play?" There are three possibilities for you: leader, supporter, or observer.

1. *Leader.* You usually play this role with an inexperienced rep. You basically run the whole call while the rep takes notes and soaks up information. As a leader, you're engaging in directive learning. Tell the rep, "After the call, I'm going to test you in these key areas. Watch how I introduce myself and build rapport, then bridge into the business topic. Take note of the questions I ask, how I gather information from the customer, and how I use my questions to control the sale. And then watch for how I close for the commitment." After the call, quiz the rep about what you did, and ask, "What are you going to do differently on your next call, based on what you saw here?"

2. *Supporter.* Your role is to add bits of information, and to step in to get a wandering rep back on track. In this case, you want the rep to lead the call. In most cases, you're the supporter for a semiexperienced rep you want to help get a feel for the sales cycle and your business. Let the rep know you may be stepping in once in a while to readjust the presentation or questioning techniques.

3. *Observer.* Remember that your goal is to make your quota through your people, not for them. When it gets to the point where you can travel on a call just to observe and not step in, then you've succeeded in your job as a manager—to train reps to sell in their own style, handling

the call with the basic techniques of selling. This is a manager's greatest reward: to watch his training and coaching come to life through an increasingly successful sales rep.

After the call

Always start with aspects of the call that went well, then question the rep in a way that makes him bring up the problems he saw during the call. Ask your rep how he thinks the call went. Get the rep to bring up areas where he thinks he can improve, and how he thinks he might achieve that improvement. You can then encourage him by reinforcing what he did right in the call.

★ **Use the royal "we."** Don't overwhelm the rep with too much criticism and too many suggestions. Pick one or two areas that you feel will have the greatest impact on the rep's performance, and save the others for later. Using of the royal "we" can take the sting out of a lot of criticism. "What could *we* have done differently on this call?" implies a team approach to finding solutions.

   If the rep still doesn't see the problem area, you might say, "Remember when the customer was telling us about her needs in the shipping department? What could we have asked that would have gotten us more information?"

★ **Give your feedback immediately after the call.** Don't wait for end-of-the-month performance reviews. When you get back to the office, transfer your notes from the call and the feedback session onto a Coaching Form (see page 106). The form serves three purposes:

1. Every time you go on a call with a rep, you can look back at the previous form and evaluate progress.

2. When it's time for performance reviews, you have a documented track record to rely on.

3. If it's necessary to let someone go, you have the facts to back up your decision.

☆ **Follow up the in-field observation with a letter or memo, and another in-field observation.** After each in-field observation, reiterate the things you talked about in the evaluation—both positive and negative. Tell the rep to keep you posted on her progress, and that if she has any questions about anything you discussed, she should feel free to ask.

Follow-up is probably the most important part of coaching sales reps in the field. If you travel with a rep, give her feedback, listen to her comments, lay out an action plan—and if you forget about it, nothing will have been accomplished. You must measure changes. This means talking to the rep several times after the call to ask how the action plan is working, and going out in the field with her again to see results firsthand.

The Coaching Form

The following Coaching Form is provided as an outline (or a template for you to recreate on your computer) to use either during a call or immediately afterwards to make notes about the sales rep's performance. The entire form does not have to be filled out while you're on the call with the rep. The information can be transferred onto this form from notes you take in the field.

You can also give a copy of the completed form to the sales rep as feedback. Be sure, however, to include strengths as well as weaknesses. Always look for the good in your sales rep, even if it's just to praise her for being able to get the call in the first place.

The coaching form is important documentation for you to have as a record of fact in case problems arise leading to termination, and as a measuring tool to rate the rep's performance levels.

Coaching Form

Salesperson: _____

Date: _____

Customer Observed: _____

Observations	Strengths	Areas for Improvement:
Ability to Build Rapport		
Qualifying and Questioning Skills		
Listening Skills		
Presentation		
Handling Objections		
Gaining Commitment		
Suggested Questions to Ask Rep After Sales Call	1 or 2 priority deficiencies for rep to focus on	

10 Steps to Successful Counseling

After coaching a rep on a particular behavior or selling skill, give it time to sink in. If you see no improvement after a few weeks, or only temporary improvement, repeat the coaching. If repeated coaching fails, counseling is the next step. Here are the 10 steps you can take for an effective counseling session:

1. **Choose a quiet, private space.** Make sure to find an area where you won't be interrupted, and set aside enough time in your schedule. If possible, stay away from your office where the phone may ring and people may knock at your door. This not only gives you privacy, it shows that this individual is important to you, and that you're willing to put time aside just for her.

2. **Prepare an outline of key points you want to cover.** Take your coaching forms with you, and any other written documentation you may have. Note clearly any skill deficiencies and/or problems you've noticed, and also any areas **that** need improvement.

3. **Start out on a positive note.** Don't belabor the point; the rep knows this is a counseling session, not an admiration society meeting. But also remember that you're not trying to make the rep feel like a total failure. You're trying to resolve a particular problem.

4. **Set up an open problem-solving environment.** Make sure that you and the rep understand the problem in the same way, and are speaking the "same language." Let her know that this is something you'd like to work out together.

For instance, you might say, "Our goal today is to talk about a few areas that need improvement, and I want you to help me out. I think you have excellent potential; that's why I hired you. My goal is to find out what I can do to help you go further, and what's stopping us from moving on to higher levels."

5. **Set open-ended questions.** Allow the rep to explain her side of the situation. An effective counselor uses questions the same way a salesperson does—to get the individual to open up and let you know what's going on so. That way, you and the rep can take the necessary steps to move on.

6. **Support your evaluations with documentation.** This serves as a reminder both to you and to the rep of specific occasions during which the problem was visible. It also stops the rep from denying events that actually occurred.

7. **Get the salesperson's agreement on areas that need improvement.** Ask, "Do you see how this is important for you?" As soon as the rep admits there is a problem, you've gotten over the toughest part. Make sure she understands what's been said during the counseling session, and that she knows what steps need to be taken.

8. **Guide, don't push.** Throughout the session, let the rep come up with as many solutions as possible. If you have answers for everything and put words in her mouth, the rep will feel she's been pushed into a corner. It's easy to tell people what to do; it's more difficult to

help them come up with answers that will work for them.

9. **Summarize and review.** Go back over key points. Include items you brought up, as well as the rep's own suggestions and plans for improvement. Let the rep know what the consequences are if the goals set at this session are not met. Give her a time frame in which improvements are to be made.

10. **Have the rep commit to an action plan.** Ask her to come up with a one-page list of some of the changes she can start making in the next two weeks. If she comes up with a plan herself, she's more likely to use it. If it's not realistic, you can always make adjustments.

Counseling Action Plan

On page 110 is an example of an action plan for you to use during your counseling session, with explanations for each section. On the next page, you'll find a blank form for you to copy and use.

Introduction and Overview: (How are you going to start the session? What positives are you going to mention? How are you going to state the problems?)

Suggested questions to start the meeting: (Use open-ended questions that will get the rep talking.)
1.
2.
3.
4.

Observations in the field, office, and after hours that relate to deficiencies:

Employee's comments: (Any explanation or commitment to action the rep made.)

Action Plan: Follow-up Dates:
Role-play: Assign with other reps in a sales meeting.

Assigned reading or tapes: Look for ones specifically related to his problem, if possible.

Travel assignment: Pair rep with more experienced salesperson (he may pick up more from peers than manager).

Assign meeting topic: Give him a topic to present during a sales meeting (see next session for details).

Prepare presentation or demonstration: Give him practice and increase his product knowledge.

Assign research: Have the rep research companies on the Internet to generate new leads.

Activity goals: Give the rep specific targets to shoot for.

Counseling Action Plan

Introduction and Overview:

Suggested questions to start the meeting:
1.
2.
3.
4.

Observations in the field, office, and after hours that relate to deficiencies:

Employee's comments:

Action Plan: Follow-up Dates:
Role-play:

Assigned reading or tapes:

Travel assignment:

Assign meeting topic:

Prepare presentation or demonstration:

Assign research:

Activity goals:

Performance Improvement Plan

If we put 100 percent effort into coaching and counseling the sales rep and don't see any improvement, or at least an effort to improve, it might be time to put the rep on probation. Here's where changes are no longer suggestions—they are mandates. If no improvement is made within a specified time limit, the employee will be let go. Many companies are lenient when it comes to probationary time frames, giving as much as two months for improvements to show. The problem with that is, the rep will probably spend those two months looking for another job. If possible, give reps no more than a month to show measurable results. Make your performance improvement plan SMART:

Specific: Identify what particular areas need improvement, such as product knowledge, or cold calls.

Measurable: Make sure your action plan will make improvements you can actually see within a month.

Attainable: Make sure your improvement plan is realistic.

Rewarding: Tap into what's most important to this particular rep so that he's motivated to change.

Timed: Let the rep know exactly how much time she has to make any necessary improvements.

On page 113 you'll find a Performance Improvement Plan, which you can eith copy onto plain paper or as a template in your computer.

Performance Improvement Plan

Sales Rep's Name _____

Date: _____

Length of Probation: ___/___/____ to ___/___/_____

Background Information on Sales Rep:

Documented Notes from Coaching Form:

Probation Activities:

- ☐ Activity deficiency
- ☐ Skill deficiency
- ☐ Knowledge
- ☐ Attitude

Explain:

Program Outline:

Results:

The Decision to Terminate

There are times when, after coaching and counseling an employee for several months, it's difficult to remain objective. The rep may be on the borderline—you're not sure whether to keep working with him or to let him go. The following suggestions may help you make this difficult decision.

Measure your own efforts

Have you tried as much as possible to help this rep? Have you paid attention to his individual goals and needs? Do you know if there are any personal problems influencing his performance at the moment?

There is a balance in the degree of effort a sales manager puts into working with his reps, and the level of return of that effort. If a sales manager really cares about the team and puts 110 percent effort into working with the reps, you'll usually see a parallel effort by the reps, because they don't want to let the manager down.

Measure specific factors

There are six main factors to look at when making a termination decision. They are the sales rep's:

1. Attitude.
2. Effort.
3. Effect on team morale.
4. Potential.
5. Performance history.
6. Ethics.

Utilize pre-termination options

Suppose you've been working with a rep and he's not responding to coaching and counseling. What are your options? You can:

✮ Have the rep run a sales meeting on the topic in which he's deficient.

✮ Send him on joint calls with other reps who are more experienced and who are proficient in areas this rep is deficient.

✮ Review his MAP board and set up an action plan based on specific areas he needs to improve.

✮ Put him on probation and give him exact numbers he has to hit to stay on board.

✮ Fire him.

Don't make a sudden decision

A rep may make you frustrated, resentful, or angry. You may observe a bad attitude or lack of effort and want to fire the rep on the spot. However, termination should be based on long-term performance criteria rather than snap judgments. The only time termination is carried out swiftly is when there has been an illegal act or serious breach of ethics.

Review Sales Rep Analysis Worksheet

When you're having a rough time deciding whether to fire a rep, the best idea is to sit down with your supervisor or with a peer manager not directly involved with this rep. Go over the following key points so you can make an objective decision:

1. **Time on the job.** How long has the employee been with you?

2. **Background experience.** Where did this rep come from before he took this job? What in his background made you hire him?

3. **Observation (in the field, in the office, or after hours).** What notes have you made about

---

115

this rep's behavior and professional performance? Any observation in less formal situations, such as after-hour socializing?

4. **Deficiencies.** What skills is he lacking? What knowledge? Why is he failing?

5. **Achievement/History.** What are the positive notes about this rep? What is his success track record?

6. **Potential.** How far do you think this rep can actually go? (Circle one: 1=poor, 10=excellent.)

   1 2 3 4 5 6 7 8 9 10

7. **Coaching, counseling, and performance improvement plan.** How much coaching and counseling has been done? Has he been on a performance improvement plan before? Were any other steps taken to try to help the rep improve?

8. **Effort.** How much effort have you as a sales manager put into training and improving this rep? (Circle one. 1=no effort, 10=a lot effort.)

   1 2 3 4 5 6 7 8 9 10

   Additional information: List other areas of training and support given to this rep.

9. **Knowing what you know now, would you re-hire this person?** If the answer is no, it probably means you're leaning towards termination.

10. **Develop an action plan.** If you determine that the rep still has potential, your partner should be able to give you some new insight and ideas on how to get this person back on track.

Sales Rep Analysis Worksheet

Time on the job:

Background experience:

Observation (in the field, in the office, after hours):

Deficiencies:

Achievement/history:

Potential: (Circle one. 1=poor, 10=excellent.)

1 2 3 4 5 6 7 8 9 10

Coaching:

Counseling:

Performance Imoprovement Plan:

Other:

How much effort have you, as a sales manager put into training and improving this rep? (Circle one. 1=no effort, 10=a lot effort.)

1 2 3 4 5 6 7 8 9 10

Additional information:

Knowing what you know now, would you rehire this person?

Action plan.

The Benefits of Firing a Problem Rep

A sales manager's credibility is an important factor in his ability to lead the team. If you constantly let reps get away with mediocre performance—making only 40 to 50 percent of quota—you're sending a distinct message to the rest of the team. The people who are making 70 to 80 percent of quota will feel they can rest on their laurels if the poorer performers are not being fired. Here are some advantages of clearing out problem personnel once every effort has been made to help them.

Stop wasting time and money

If a rep is not responding, and is not even making an effort, there's no sense in continuing to spend the time and money necessary for further coaching and counseling. Both can be put to better use with other reps.

Revive the territory

A territory that has been regarded as a nonproducer may be the victim of a rep who didn't try hard enough. Once the problem rep is gone, a more experienced rep, or one with a great deal of enthusiasm, can go into the territory and repair any damage that may have been done.

Increase your own respect and credibility

Once the problem rep is fired, everyone else on the team will realize they have to live up to higher expectations. This is what happened when Michael Leiss stepped into Oce USA management in California. The reps there wanted to have Fridays off to go sailing and surfing. Liess told them, "You can have every day off if you want—if you don't want to work here." Reps must understand that the bottom line is that you're all together for one purpose: to run a business. If one person is not meeting the requirements of that business, he or she will have to be let go.

Increase overall team performance

Once the problem rep is gone, the activity and performance levels of the reps improves. They now know they have to live up to and abide by the performance expectations you set for them.

Performance Improvement Checklist

☑ **Coaching vs. Counseling. What is the difference?**

　☆　Coaching takes place on an ongoing basis, and is aimed toward a particular deficiency.

　☆　Counseling takes place when the deficiency is not corrected.

☑ **Coaching in the field—before, during, and after the sale.**

Before the call:

　☆　Ask your rep questions before you go out on the call so that you know as much as possible about the account.

　☆　Be sure the rep remains focused on his or her objective for the call.

　☆　Be sure reps have a reason to call on the customer.

　☆　Stress value-added selling.

☆ The final question to ask your rep is, "Is there anything else I should know?"

During the call:

☆ Decide which role you are going to play: leader, supporter, or observer.

After the call:

☆ Use the royal "we" during evaluation sessions.

☆ Give your feedback immediately after the call.

☆ Follow up the in-field observation with a letter or memo.

☑ **The Coaching Form.** Use the Coaching Form as a documented record of your rep's performance so that you can compare performance levels before and after training and coaching.

☑ **10 steps to successful counseling:**

1. Choose a quiet, private space.
2. Prepare an outline of key points to cover.
3. Start out on a positive note.
4. Set up an open problem-solving environment.
5. Ask open-ended questions.
6. Support your evaluations with documentation.
7. Get the salesperson's agreement on areas that need improvement.
8. Guide, don't push.
9. Summarize and review.
10. Have the rep commit to an action plan.

☑ **Counseling Action Plan.** Use this plan before and during your counseling session to keep notes for your files.

☑ **Performance Improvement Plan.** When counseling does not seem to be helping, employees may have to be put on probation. Use the Performance Improvement Plan sheet to keep notes for your files. Remember to make your plan SMART (see page 112).

☑ **The decision to terminate.** Here are some suggestions to help you make this difficult decision:

1. Measure your own effort.
2. Measure specific factors.
3. Consider pre-termination options.
4. Don't make a sudden decision.

☑ **Use the Sales Rep Analysis Worksheet.** Find an objective partner who can help you review the employee's history and make the decision. Here are the key decision-influencing points:

1. Time on the job.
2. Background experience.
3. Observations from the field, office, and after hours.
4. Deficiencies.
5. Achievement history.
6. Potential.
7. Coaching, counseling, and Performance Improvement Plan history.
8. How much effort has already gone into training and counseling?
9. Would you rehire?
10. Action plan.
11. The benefits of firing a problem rep.
12. Stop wasting time and money.
13. Revive the territory.
14. Increase your own respect and credibility.
15. Increase overall team performance.

CHAPTER 7

RUNNING
EFFECTIVE
SALES MEETINGS

There is nothing more boring than a badly run sales meeting. The kind where the manager comes in with no particular agenda, and says, "So, what's happening? I just wanted us all to get together. Anybody have any questions about the new product line?" If nobody has any questions, the manager proceeds to speak about unimportant matters for another 45 minutes. Half the reps are asleep and the other half are angry because they're wasting time when they could be out selling.

Of course, meetings don't have to be like this. They can be interesting, informative training sessions—a chance for you to fortify camaraderie and practice your leadership skills. Effective training happens when:

☆ **Meetings are focused.** Be sure you have a clear purpose. Meetings should cover specific topics that you have decided in advance. Don't try to squeeze too much into one session. Let the reps know what subjects are going to be covered in the meeting so that they can come prepared with questions and their own insight into the topic.

★ **Meetings are interactive.** No one likes to listen to a lecture—and people don't learn well from them, either. We learn best from doing. Whether you set up role-plays, hold contests, or have reps give brief presentations, activity generates energy and excitement, and also makes it easier to learn and remember skills and concepts.

★ **Managers prepare.** "Winging it" in a sales meeting will not produce desired results. Meetings are meant to be training sessions in areas where reps need help. Ask each rep to make a list of three or four topics they'd like to have covered in meetings.

★ **The emphasis is on practical information.** Reps may be coming in early for these meetings, or staying on their own personal time. You have to make the meeting worth their while. Be sure the information you're imparting is practical, not theoretical. Reps want to learn skills they can put to use immediately.

★ **Meetings are run with passion and enthusiasm.** The word enthusiasm comes from the Greek word enthos which means "the God within." If you're trying to sell an idea to your reps, your greatest sales tool is your own enthusiasm and belief in what you're doing.

★ **Meetings end with a call to action.** When the meeting is over, everyone should have a clear idea of what is expected of them in the near future. If the purpose of the meeting is to introduce a new product, for example, reps should be assigned to give a minidemonstration of that product at the next meeting.

✱ **You are creative.** Use audiotapes, videotapes, computer games,music,brainteasers, puzzles—anything that makes the meeting fun and challenging at the same time.

✱ **There is good follow-up.** Get out into the field with reps and observe whether the skills you're teaching are being retained and utilized. If they're not, find out why.

The 4 T's of Presentation

The rules of presentation for a sales meeting are the same rules you use when making presentations to customers. There is a pattern you can follow to guarantee a successful presentation. First, before you tell them what you're going to tell them, tell them *why* you're telling them what you're going to tell them. Then, follow the 4 T's of presentations:

1. **Tell them what you're going to tell them.** Your "audience" will follow you much more willingly if they sense you know where you're going. So you might open your presentation with a statement like, "What I'm going to do today is take you through the goals of a successful sales call, the 10 best qualifying questions, and gaining commitment through trial closing." Now, you've got them waiting to hear the information you've got. Then, tell them *why* they need this information: "This will help us tremendously in areas where we're not getting the right information on the sales call and we're losing business to our competitors."

2. **Tell them.** Go through your presentation, following the outline you proposed earlier. Be brief, yet passionate. Let your reps know that what you have to say is important. Keep your thoughts clear and succinct, and present your ideas in a logical sequence.

3. **Test them.** Powerful presentations, like good meetings, are interactive. You want to keep your listeners involved. You want to stay in control of the presentation, but you also want to get your reps' input. Ask questions that will get you feedback. You want to know: Is the presentation hitting home? Does it make sense? Is it addressing their needs and concerns?

4. **Tell them what you told them.** Summarize your ideas so that the presentation is focused: "What we just looked at was the new product line from Widgets, Inc., and the four key ways these products can help grow our customers' businesses. Did you see how we can sell the new product line as an adjunct to the Widgets they may already have?"

Planning a Training Session

Planning a training session is divided into three sections: Premeeting assignments, the actual session, and postmeeting assignments.

Pre-meeting assignments

Premeeting assignments can be very useful motivational tools. They also help reps become proficient in areas where they may have had deficiencies. By giving out these assignments a week or two before the meeting, it gets the reps thinking about the proposed topic, and any questions they may want to ask. Some suggested topics for pre-assignment include:

⭐ **Handling objections.** Ask your reps to bring to the meeting five of their most common objections and the way they handle them now. Get them thinking about those objections beforehand, and they'll probably start changing the way they handle them before they even get to the meeting!

⭐ **Prospecting techniques.** Ask your reps to be prepared to demonstrate a particular product. Put slips of paper with the names of various features in a hat, and during the meeting each rep will pick one. The rep will have to demonstrate that feature to the rest of the group. Because the reps don't know which feature they'll pull from the hat, they'll have to be prepared to demonstrate the entire product.

⭐ **Breaking into major accounts.** Ask your reps for the five largest accounts they would like to break into in their territory. Have them bring any information they have to the meeting, and be prepared to strategize ways to get these accounts.

⭐ **Selling value.** Ask your reps to bring to the meeting five reasons why customers should pay more for your product.

What you're actually doing is forcing reps to realize that they're going to be involved in the meeting. At the same time, you're stimulating their thinking on these subjects. Use the sheet on page 129 for written assignments.

Sales Meeting Outline

Develop a broad outline of the training session you are about to conduct. An outline sheet for you to use during your planning stages is on page 130. A blank sheet for you to copy and use is on page 131.

Post-meeting assignment

It is critical that each meeting end with a postmeeting assignment. Reps should walk out of the meeting with a specific assignment for the week ahead. If the topic of your meeting has been qualifying questions, for example, you can end the meeting by saying, "Use all the questions we talked about when you go out in the field this week. Next week we're going to talk about which of these questions worked best for you."

Follow up these assignments in the field

Be on the lookout for the topics and techniques discussed at the meeting, and how they're working for the individual rep. Then, at the next meeting, decide what you are going to use to measure the results reps report. (Did they make more cold calls? More qualified calls? Did demonstrations result in more sales?)

Premeeting Assignment Sheet

To: _____

Meeting date: _____

Meeting topic(s): _____

_____

_____

Please prepare the following: _____

_____

_____

_____

_____

_____

_____

_____

_____

_____

_____

_____

Sales Meeting Outline

Subject: _____

Meeting date: _____

Time: _____

Objectives

At the end of the meeting, the sales reps will be able to:

Each meeting should have a specific objective, such as how to handle three of the most common objections, or five new ways to break into large accounts. Write down specific results you'd like to see at the end of this meeting. This way, at the end of the meeting, you can look down at the paper and ask yourself, "Did I accomplish this objective?"

Premeeting assignments:

Which reps were given assignments for this meeting?

What were their assignments?

Post-meeting assignments:

What am I going to ask people to do during the week after the meeting?

What am I going to ask people to bring to the next meeting?

Others attending:

Guest speaker: _____

Service: _____

Customer: _____

Other: _____

Sales Meeting Outline

Subject: _____

Meeting date: _____

Time: _____

Objectives

At the end of the meeting, the sales reps will be able to:

Premeeting assignments:

Postmeeting assignments:

Others attending:

Guest speaker: _____

Service: _____

Customer: _____

Other: _____

Meeting Schedule

Time	Topic	Speaker
: to :		
: to :		
: to :		
: to :		
: to :		
: to :		
: to :		
: to :		

Follow-up

Follow-up Plan (in Field)
Next Meeting (Measure Results)

Setting Meeting Results

Once the meeting begins, it is your obligation to be sure that both you and the participants understand the objectives of the meeting. To be sure that happens, here are some suggested techniques:

Outline program contents

Let the reps know what this meeting is about, focusing on the desired results. For example, you might say, "At the end of today's meeting, you will be able to handle the most common objections we receive on the Widget line."

Post the objectives on the wall

There may be three or four different subjects to be covered in the meeting. List these objectives, and post the list on the wall in full view of all the participants.

Tie participants' expectations into the program content

In other words, if the subject for the meeting is handling objections, go around the room and ask each person for one idea of what they would like to see covered during the meeting. You want to find out what they expect from the meeting. You're doing a "needs analysis" of the group to make sure the presentation is tailored to fit their needs. During the meeting you can say, for example, "You mentioned as part of your expectations that you'd like to cover methods of handling objections over the phone. We're now going to discuss three steps to make that process easier."

Post the expectations on the wall next to the program objectives

You want the participants to be able to see what you've planned to cover and what they want to have covered. It also keeps you on track during the meeting so you remember to tie those two aspects together.

Make sure the training is measurable

Keep testing the participants throughout the meeting via role-plays, discussions, and written exercises. You want to be sure that they understand what is being taught. There's no way for you to know that unless you get the reps involved.

Meeting Management

If meetings are to be taken seriously, they must have an agenda that both you and the participants follow. Reps should know that you keep your promises. You start when you say you will—not after 15 minutes of small talk and coffee—and you won't let the meeting drag on and on. Here are some suggestions for running a smooth, efficient meeting:

Start the meeting on time

Prepare the room and set up equipment before the participants arrive so that you can spend the first few minutes meeting and greeting—not setting up the overhead.

Give yourself leeway at the end

Tell participants that the meeting will end about 20 minutes later than you think it will. If you think you'll be through by 5 p.m., tell reps the meeting will end at 5:20. That way, if you finish at 5, everyone feels rewarded that they covered everything and can leave early as well. And if it goes a little past 5, there's no irritation.

Keep your lecturing to no more than 15 minutes at a time

If you stand up and talk in front of the group for more than 15 minutes or so, start an interactive exercise, have reps make individual or group presentations, or give out short quizzes. Constantly have reps apply the information they've just learned. Teaching is not telling. This means learning is not listening.

Don't forget to take breaks

Sales meetings are not only for learning. They are also an opportunity for team bonding. It's good to give people 15 minutes or so of unstructured time where they can catch up with their friends or peers, have a cup of coffee, and just relax. *But...*be sure to tell participants the exact time you'll be resuming the meeting. When I give seminars, I like to have fun with latecomers. If one person is late in returning, I tell all the other reps to wrinkle up a piece of paper, and when I say, "Let me be honest with you," everyone turn around and throw their paper at the latecomer. It's good for a laugh, but it also gets the point across: Don't be late the next time, or you will be the target of a practical joke. (The only time I'll do this is when I have an excellent rapport with the group.) What usually happens is that the reps rush back in after the next break because no one wants to be the latecomer this time.

Keep the meeting under control

It's easy to get off on tangents. People often ask questions that derail your train of thought. If someone does ask a question that's off the topic, you might say, "That's an excellent question, and we're going to get to that in the next module. Why don't you make a note of that thought and remind me if I don't cover it after the break." Keep checking your objectives and expectations charts to note where you are and how much is left to be covered. If a discussion is going on too long, you might say, "We can take one more question on this and then we're going to have to move on."

Use the 4 Ts of presentations

Of course, that applies to the meeting as a whole. But it also applies to each section of the meeting. Go over the four Ts before the program starts, before the break, when you start again after the break, and before the meeting ends. For instance, you might say, "Let's take a look at what we covered this morning... When we come back from the break we'll go into..." When the meeting resumes, you begin by saying, "We just covered the four methods of.... What we're going to cover now is..." This technique gives the meeting structure and reinforces the important points that were covered and the important points to be covered.

Questioning Techniques to Get Your People Involved

No matter what type of meeting it is, the manager's role—and the most critical part of any training—is to get participants involved. The easiest, most efficient way to do this is to ask questions.

The benefits of group involvement

✸ *It improves creativity and learning.* Reps are thinking and doing, they're not just listening. Activity promotes higher retention of information.

✸ *Reps learn from their peers.* The more everyone is involved, the more opportunity for everyone to learn from each other.

✸ *It helps the manager understand the group's current knowledge of the subject under discussion.* If the group is very knowledgeable in one area of the subject, spend less time on that than you had originally planned, and move on to areas where there's a greater need for training.

136

✭ *It builds the leader's credibility.* When you access the group's key needs and tailor your program toward them, then any recommendations you make will have a strong focus and foundation.

Always start the meeting with a general question

Start off with a basic open-ended question you know everyone can answer. For instance, you might say, "The first subject we're going to cover today is qualifying. What is qualifying, anyway?" This immediately lets people know you're not going to give them all the answers; they're going to have to become involved.

Use direct questions to get individuals to open up

Suppose nobody answers the opening question. You then choose someone you know can answer the question: "Bob, what's your definition of qualifying?" Ask directed questions to a few people at the start of the meeting. This accomplishes several things:

✭ It gets immediate involvement from members of the group.

✭ It puts people on their toes, and lets them know they're going to have to listen because they might be called on at any moment.

✭ It allows you to give recognition to reps in front of their peers. Always compliment a rep's feedback so that you build his confidence and make him want to talk more. If the answer is not so good, say, "Interesting point. Does anyone else have a comment on that?" By passing the question on, you don't embarrass the rep or argue with him in front of his peers. If you do, you'll usually lose that rep for the rest of the meeting.

137

Transfer questions back to the group

Sometimes reps expect you to have all the answers. They ask questions such as, "What's the best way to handle price objections?" The truth is, there is no "best" way; reps need to find ways that work for them. Follow up that question with: "What are some of the methods you've used?" Then, "Anybody else have any other ideas?" You've transferred the question back to the group. A lot of people know more than they think they do, and you can bring it out of them.

Don't argue with the challenges

There may be someone in the group who disagrees with something you've said. They say, "That won't work for my customers (or this type of product, or in this industry, etc.)" Never argue, even if the challenger is a rep who wants to upstage you. Answer the challenge with a question: "Why do you feel that way? What specifically won't work in your situation?" If he's got a good point, give him credit for it. But ask the rest of the group: "How do the rest of you feel about that?" They may come up with ways to challenge the challenger.

Creating a Workshop Environment

There are some reps who are extremely resistant to meetings and training. Most of the time, that's because they're nervous about having to "perform" in front of their peers. They don't want to be called on to give a demonstration or role-play in front of the group. Here are some methods for solving this problem.

Create a nonthreatening atmosphere

Let people know they are there to learn, not to be humiliated or embarrassed. Let them know they're going to be learning, but that they're going to have fun as well.

138

Do some exercises where you can pair people up so that everyone is working simultaneously, rather than having one or two people exposed in front of the group.

Let participants know mistakes are encouraged

Sometimes people won't answer questions because they're afraid of giving a wrong answer. From the beginning, let the reps know that this is the place to make mistakes. You might say, "I'd rather you make your mistakes here in front of us instead of out in the field where it's going to cost us money." Remind them that there's no such thing as a stupid question.

Let your enthusiasm show

Be passionate about the subject, whatever it is. You have to believe that what you're discussing will help your people to be their best. It's the only way you can get your reps excited about learning what it is you have to teach. Remember that enthusiasm is the single most important factor in selling your reps on the training program.

Use your own experiences to enliven the meeting

It's not necessary to go into hours and hours of your own personal war stories. But reps like to know that you've been there before them, that you have the credentials to be teaching them how to sell.

Be prepared and professional

Sales meetings and training seminars are no place to wing it. When participants see that you're thoroughly prepared, they respect you more and are ready to get down to business.

Setting Up the Training Room

The physical environment in which a meeting is held can have a great influence on whether that meeting is successful. The setup must fit the number of participants and the meeting style you have in mind. There are four basic room setups.

Classroom style

It's called classroom style because that's what it looks like: rows of seats, one behind the other, with the leader standing in front of the room. This works best for large groups, sometimes in actual classrooms or auditoriums. In this setup, which should only be used for 50 people or more, group discussions or pairing-off exercises are difficult, if not impossible.

Table groups

This is the best setup for groups of 12 to 50 participants. If there are 20 participants, for example, the room would be set up with four tables of five. Each table is a team, and each team chooses a leader. Then if you ask a question such as, "What are the best questions to ask on a first call?" each group has their own discussion and writes their answers on a flip chart. Next, go around the room and ask each team leader for his or her group's answers. This setup invites interaction because people are immediately working in teams. It's good for team-building, and it also creates a healthy competition between teams.

Horseshoe

This shape should be limited to about 20 participants. Any more than that, and you can't walk into the center of the group without "losing" the people on the left and right sides of the table.

Round table

This setup, which should be limited to about eight people, creates an atmosphere of equality between participants and encourages open discussion.

It is often helpful to have flip charts stationed at each table to have the participants post their ideas after brainstorming different topics. Another great advantage of flip charts is the ability to tear them off and post on the wall around the training room. This allows the individuals to see all topics that were worked on during the meeting.

The worst nightmare for an audience is to sit through 50 overheads with 20 bullets on each page. Make sure whatever media you're using to convey your message is brief, easy to read, and, if possible, colorful.

Dealing With Problem Participants

Sometimes the most well-prepared managers run into trouble in the form of problem participants. You don't want to argue with, confront, or embarrass them in front of their peers. Yet they can't be ignored, either, or they can ruin an otherwise productive training session and make it difficult for everyone else present to concentrate and learn. Here are three problem types and how to deal with them.

The shy one

Although this person doesn't affect the rest of the group that much, you still want to draw a shy rep out. Training works best when everyone participates, and you want the shy rep to learn as much as the others. Ask a shy rep a direct question that you know he can answer. Call his name first so that he can "get ready" to answer. Instead of saying, "Who can give me the definition of a cold call? Steve?" Say, "Steve, what is your definition of a cold call?" Don't stand too close when asking a question, speak softly, and be sure to compliment him on his answer.

The talker

Then there are the opposites of the shy ones—the people who want to answer every question, and who take 1,000 words to answer a close-ended question. When this happens, stand directly behind the talker; it's guaranteed to make him uncomfortable. Walk to the opposite side of the room, and interrupt the talker if necessary by saying, "Let's hear from some other people. Steve, what do you think?" If you simply let the talker go on, you'll lose control of the meeting and it may be difficult to get it back.

The egotist

Sometimes you get a rep in a meeting who feels she knows it all, and that this kind of training is a waste of time. This personality can be disruptive, but it can also be seen as challenge. There are two types of ego personalities. The first is the number one performer on the team who really does know what she's talking about, and deserves to be proud of it. You want to get this rep on your side. When you get resistance from her, use the turnaround. Ask her, "Joan, how would you do this differently?" If she has a valid point, praise her for it, give her recognition in front of her peers, because that's what she's craving. However, if she's interrupting the group's learning ability, take her aside during the break. You might say, "Joan, I appreciate your input and all your comments are great. People love to hear your ideas. I just want to give some other reps a chance to answer some questions, so if I cut you off, don't take it personally."

This personality type often ends up being the best student, if you know how to manage her. If her comments are good, I'll refer to them throughout my presentation. If she's made a point about qualifying, for example, I might say, "Remember what Joan said before? She made an excellent point about getting others in the company involved." I take her comment, tie it into what I'm saying, and then Ms. Ego becomes my friend. I don't want to fight with her. If I do, the others in the group will naturally side with their peer. Then I've lost control of the whole group.

The second ego personality is usually someone who's been around, but has no great track record or authority. You might try calling his bluff. If he challenges you on a particular topic, ask him to come up front and make a presentation to the group about it. If he knows what he's talking about, the group will learn from it. If not, the group will see through him, and he'll back off.

Postmeeting Follow-Up

Once again, the follow-up is the most important part of the process. The feedback you get from your reps not only helps you evaluate them, it helps you evaluate the effectiveness of your training, and how to plan for the next meeting or training seminar.

End-of-the-meeting evaluation

At the close of the meeting, you want to be able to measure the results of your training. Go around the room and ask each participant to tell you one thing they're going to do differently as a result of the meeting. This allows you to see how much the group has learned, and what was most important to them.

Training Follow-Up Report

Motivation to change is highest directly after the meeting is over. You want to know if that motivation has continued, and if the training is being applied in the field. Approximately two weeks after the training is over, hand

out or e-mail this questionnaire to the program participants and ask them to fill it out and return it to you.

Training Follow-Up Report

1. What are you doing *now* that you were not doing
before the last sales meeting?

2. How many sales have you made that you can attribute directly to the sales training you received?
Please explain.

3. What step of the sales cycle are you having the most
difficulty with?

4. If a follow-up workshop were offered relating to this
topic, what would you like to see covered?

Effective Meetings Checklist

☑ **Effective training happens when...**

   ☆ Meetings are focused.

   ☆ Meetings are interactive.

   ☆ Managers prepare.

   ☆ The emphasis is on practical information.

   ☆ Meetings are run with passion and enthusiasm.

   ☆ Meetings end with a call to action.

   ☆ There is good follow-up.

☑ **The 4 Ts of presentations**

   ☆ Tell them what you're going to tell them.

   ☆ Tell them.

   ☆ Test them.

   ☆ Tell them what you told them.

☑ **Planning a training session**

   ☆ Give reps a premeeting assignment.

   ☆ Develop a broad outline for the actual sales meeting, including your objective and the results you want to see when the meeting is over.

   ☆ Give reps postmeeting assignments.

   ☆ Follow up these assignments in the field.

☑ **Setting meeting objectives**

   ☆ Outline program content.

   ☆ Post the objective on the wall.

- ☆ Tie participants' expectations into the program content.
- ☆ Post the expectations on the wall next to the program objectives.
- ☆ Make sure the training is measurable.

☑ **Meeting management**
- ☆ Start the meeting on time.
- ☆ Give yourself leeway at the end.
- ☆ Keep lecturing to no more than 15 minutes at a time.
- ☆ Don't forget to take breaks.
- ☆ Keep the meeting under your control.
- ☆ Use the four Ts of presentation.
- ☆ Give participants updated agendas as the meeting goes on.

☑ **Questioning techniques to get participants involved**
The benefits of group involvement include:
- ☆ Improved creativity and learning.
- ☆ Reps learn from their peers.
- ☆ It helps the manager understand the group's current knowledge of the subject.
- ☆ It builds the leader's credibility. Always start with a general question.
- ☆ Use direct questions to get individuals to open up.
- ☆ Transfer questions back to the group.
- ☆ Don't argue with challenges.

☑ **Create a workshop environment**
- ☆ Create a nonthreatening atmosphere.

☆ Let participants know mistakes are encouraged.

☆ Let your enthusiasm show.

☆ Use your own experiences to enliven the meeting.

☆ Be prepared and professional.

☑ **Setting up the training room**

☆ Classroom style: leader in front, with rows of seats behind (50 people or more).

☆ Table groups: tables set up around the room with several participants at each (12 to 50 participants).

☆ Horseshoe: semicircle (less than 20 participants).

☆ Round table: circular seating (limited to about 8 people).

☑ **How to deal with problem participants**

☆ The shy ones: Ask questions from a distance, speak softly, and direct questions to them using their name.

☆ The talkers: Stand directly behind them, and interrupt if necessary.

☆ Egotists: Try to get this rep as your ally. Explain that although he knows the answers, he can help by letting others participate as well.

☑ **Postmeeting follow-up**

☆ End-of-the-meeting evaluation. Have everyone state the most important point they learned at the meeting, and how they'll make changes in the field.

☑ **Training Follow-Up Report**

☆ Two weeks after the training, ask these questions:

1. What are you doing *now* that you were not doing before the last sales meeting?

2. How many sales have you made that you can attribute directly to the sales training you received? Please explain.

3. What step of the sales cycle are you having the most difficulty with?

4. If a follow-up workshop were offered relating to this topic, what would you like to see covered?

AFTERWORD

This book started out with a description of the sales manager everyone hates to work for. Applying the principles you've read throughout these chapters will assure that you never fall into that category. Those principles have given you insight into the three most important skills a manager will possess: the ability to hire the right people; to train, counsel and coach them; and to keep them constantly motivated.

These are not skills that are used once and then discarded. They're part of a manager's everyday existence. Hiring, training, and motivation are ongoing processes. Use this book as a reference guide to keep learning and improving these skills.

Use it to remind yourself that you should always be looking for new talent to hire and develop, to make sure you're asking the most effective interview questions to measure motivation before you hire, and to use the key success factors from top performers as reminders of the qualities you're looking for in a new hire.

Keep the five major goals of a sales manager in mind:

1. Make quota constantly.
2. Operate at a profit.
3. Grow and expand the business.
4. Build a strong team.
5. Self-development.

Spend time with your people. Fine-tune your evaluation skills in the field and in the office. Set up systems for monitoring reps' activity levels, and let them know clearly what's expected of them. Know that there may be times when the best choice for the company and for the team may be to let someone go—that you sacrifice your time with other reps by constantly trying to work with someone who isn't going to change. Use the knowledge you've gained from spending time with your reps to create a motivating environment and to design sales meetings that are interesting and informative.

And finally, to be the sales manager everyone loves to work for.

I'd be happy to hear from you with any comments or ideas you'd like to share. Write to me at:

Farber Training Systems
66 East Sherbrooke Parkway
Livingston, NJ 07039
Or you can e-mail me at barry@barryfarber.com.
Be sure to visit my Website at *www.barryfarber.com*.

INDEX

R

Recognition, 57-58, 82
Recruiting techniques,
26-32, 44
Reference checks, 41-42, 46
Resumes, 32-33, 45
Cover Sheet, 33-34, 45

S

Sales Call
coaching after, 104-105, 120
coaching before, 100-102,
119-120
coaching during,
103-104, 120
Sales Managers, 15-23
goals, 51-54
roles, 49-71
successful, traits of a
19-22, 50
unfavorable, profile of a
16-18
Sales Manager's Checklist,
69-71
Sales Rep Analysis
Worksheet, 115-117, 121
Sales Reps, key success
factors for, 42-43, 46-47
Self-development, 53-54, 69

Selling, value-added, 102
Software, sales, 91-95, 97

T

Team
performance, 119
strengthening of, 53, 69
Techniques, prospecting, 127
Technology, 77-78, 91-97
Technology, time
management and, 87-98
Telephone prescreen, 29-30
Time Management and
Technology Checklist,
96-97
Time Management Test, 88-89
Time management, 87-91
Training Follow-Up Report,
143-144, 148
Training
room, setting up a, 140-141
session, planning a,
126-132, 145-148

W

War room, 59, 78
Work Environment, creating
a motivational, 56-61, 70
Workshop environment,
138-139

ABOUT THE AUTHOR

Barry Farber is the author of eight books on sales, management, and personal achievement, including *The 12 Clichés of Selling* and *Sales Secrets From Your Customers*. He is also the president of three successful companies: Farber Training Systems, a sales and management training company; The Diamond Group, a literary agency; and Profound Products Inc., a company that creates and markets innovative products.

Well-known as a public speaker and writer, as well as a television guest and host, Barry is also a monthly columnist for *Entrepreneur*, host of *Selling Power Live*, and creator of *Focus With Farber*—a pocket magazine. He is a black belt in tae kwon do and has won awards at state, regional, and national levels in weapons competitions with a six-foot bo staff. He often uses his martial arts experience to tie into his messages on sales, marketing, and success. For more information about Barry and his products, visit *www.barryfarber.com*.